Teaching Thinking Skills with Picture Books, K-3

Teaching Thinking Skills with Picture Books

Grades K-3

Nancy Polette

Illustrated by Paul Dillon

Teacher Ideas Press

An imprint of Libraries Unlimited
Westport, Connecticut • London

Library of Congress Cataloging-in-Publication Data

Polette, Nancy.
   Teaching thinking skills with picture books, K-3 / by Nancy Polette ; illustrated by Paul
  Dillon.
    p. cm.
    Includes index.
    ISBN-13: 978-1-59158-592-3 (pbk. : alk. paper)
    1. Thought and thinking—Study and teaching (Primary) 2. Picture books for children. I.
  Title.
  LB1590.3.P654 2007
  372.13—dc22 2007016195

British Library Cataloguing in Publication Data is available.

Library of Congress Catalog Card Number: 2007016195
ISBN-13: 978-1-59158-592-3

First published in 2007

Libraries Unlimited/Teacher Ideas Press, 88 Post Road West, Westport, CT 06881
A Member of the Greenwood Publishing Group, Inc.
www.lu.com

Printed in the United States of America

♾™

The paper used in this book complies with the
Permanent Paper Standard issued by the National
Information Standards Organization (Z39.48–1984).

10 9 8 7 6 5 4 3 2 1

Contents

Introduction

Many of the most talented authors and artists of the past and present have shared their thoughts and their gifts with young children through picture books. Many picture books allow young children to explore important ideas and to stretch their minds far beyond rote memorization.

Young children absorb knowledge at a very rapid pace. In an age of information overload, it is essential that children are taught those important thinking skills that are needed in dealing with the multitude of information they meet every day. What better way to help children gain important thinking skills than exposure to quality literature.

Emphasis in 21st century schools is on testing for rote knowledge. While knowledge is the starting point, it is essential that children are taught to evaluate data, to solve problems, to make decisions based on evidence, to be able to determine cause and effect, to predict and forecast based on evidence, to support or deny a hypothesis, to infer, to interpret, to question and analyze, and to use a host of other thinking skills.

Teaching Thinking Skills with Picture Books is an easy-to-use guide to teaching those thinking skills which have been identified as appropriate for students in the primary grades. Each skill is introduced with a definition and oral practice exercise.

Quality picture books are introduced with booktalks and followed by one or more thinking skills activities. Each activity is complete and needs no other materials to use. All skills introduced can be immediately applied to other areas of curriculum, as well as to real life situations. Here is a painless approach to helping students become better thinkers with skills that will also improve reading and writing ability.

ANALOGY

An **analogy** is a comparison that points out similarities in two things that might be different in other ways.

Examples:

Ant is to anthill as bird is to nest.

Fish is to swim as bird is to _____.

STEPS:

1. Choose the items to be compared. (Fish and bird)

   Identify the connecting clue in the items. (swim)

2. Determine how the first two items are related.

   (movement)

3. Complete the analogy by choosing an item that relates to the third item (movement). Fish is to swim as bird is to fly.

ORAL PRACTICE

Puppy is to dog as kitten is to _____ (cat)

Rain is to raindrop as snow is to _____ (snowflake)

Bird is to feathers as fish is to _____ (scales)

Foot is to leg as hand is to _____ (arm)

Meow is to cat as bow wow is to _____ (dog)

Airplane is to sky as car is to _____ (road)

BOOKTALKS : THE FARM

Click Clack, Moo: Cows That Type by Doreen Cronin. Illus. by Betsy Lewin. Simon & Schuster, 2000.

Farmer Brown has a problem. His cows like to type. All day long he hears click, clack, click, clack, moo. But Farmer Brown's problems really begin when his cows start leaving him notes. They demand electric blankets because the barn is cold at night. Not only do they demand the blankets, but they refuse to give milk until they receive them.

Farmer Brown is furious and refuses to give the cows the blankets, so the cows go on strike and will not give milk. The hens, who are cold, too, join in the strike and refuse to lay eggs. Duck serves as the neutral party and takes the notes back and forth between the farmer and the cows. When the cows offer to give up their typewriter in exchange for the blankets, Farmer Brown agrees and the farm gets back to normal operation...almost!

The Mixed-Up Rooster by Pamela Duncan Edwards. Illus. by Megan Lloyd. Katherine Tegen Books, HarperCollins, 2006.

What are the hens to do with a rooster who oversleeps and does not wake up the barnyard? The hens have an egg business to run and decide to call in another rooster. Ned became a night bird playing with the bats and rabbits and tree frogs. It was then he saw a long black snake slithering towards the hen house. Long black snakes love eggs! What is Ned to do? Crow, of course, and crow he did! The snake was frightened off and the eggs were saved. As for the new rooster, he slept through it all!

Dance By the Light of the Moon by Joanne Ryder. Illus. by Guy Francis. Hyperion, 2006.

Farmer Snow is giving his annual barnyard party. The excited animals are getting ready. Buffalo Flo has an elegant bow. Gertie Goose has new shoes. Cassie Sue Cat has a flip-floppy hat. Patty Ann Pig has a pretty wig and they all come to dance by the light of the moon.

ANALOGY CUT UP

Find the missing animals below. Choose the correct animal, cut it out, and paste it in the empty box.

ANALOGY GAME

Partners cut apart the word cards and place them face down. In turn, each child chooses two cards. If there is a match the child keeps the cards. If not, the child discards one of the cards. The game continues until one player has four cards that form an analogy.

dog	bone	fish	worm
day	sun	night	moon
zoo	lion	farm	pig
tree	bird	pond	fish

ANALYSIS

Analysis refers to the breaking down of data into its basic parts based on some reason or plan. An analysis of two stories might be comparing likenesses and differences in plot, characters, settings, or themes.

STEPS:

1. Read the material to be analyzed.

2. Break the material into separate parts.

3. Discover the relationship among ideas.

4. Develop a list of facts about each relationship.

ORAL PRACTICE

1. How many ways are *Curious George* and *Clifford, the Big Red Dog* alike?

2. If Clifford were to give Curious George a present, what would it be? Why?

3. What makes *The Cat In the Hat* fun to read?

4. Analyze the pattern in *Brown Bear, Brown Bear, What Do You See?* Use the pattern to add more animals.

5. Did Max really leave his bedroom and frolic with the wild things in *Where the Wild Things Are?* Why or why not?

BOOKTALKS : HOUSES

Is This a House for Hermit Crab? by Megan McDonald. Illus. by S.D. Schindler. Orchard, 1990.

Hermit Crab is looking for a new home. Scritch, scratch, he goes along the shore, by the sea, in the sand. But each home he finds has something wrong with it. What could be wrong with a big rock? a red pail? a fishing net? a tin can? While Hermit Crab is busy searching for a home he does not see the pricklepine fish coming near. What do you suppose a pricklepine fish eats? You are right! Hermit crabs!

When Hermit Crab sees the fish, he goes "Scritch scratch, scritch scratch" as fast as he can and hides in a shell. Pricklepine fish swims around and around but can't find Hermit Crab. Finally, the fish swims away. When Hermit Crab peeks out of the shell he is happy about two things. One thing that makes him happy is that the pricklepine fish is gone. Can you guess the other?

A House Is a House for Me by Mary Ann Hoberman. Illus. by Betty Fraser. Viking Press, 1978.

What would be a house for an ant? a bee? a mole? a mouse? Do people live in different kinds of houses? What is a house for a spider? a bird? a dog? a flea? The more you think about houses the more houses you can see.

What would you find in these houses:

A husk	A sty
A pod	A hutch
A web	The ocean
A coop	

THE BEST HOUSE

Suppose Hermit Crab had not found a shell for his new home. Which of these homes might he choose? Why?

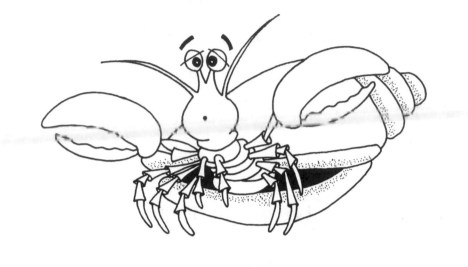

LIFE IN THE SEA

Use this pattern to write about living things in the sea. Sing to the tune of "Skip To My Lou."

Hermit crabs

Scratch, scratch, scratch

Fat jellyfish

Float, float, float

Silver dolphins

Dive, dive, dive

Living in the sea.

_____ (describing word & name)

_____ _____ _____ (what does it do?)

_____ (describing word & name)

_____ _____ _____ (what does it do?)

_____ (describing word & name)

_____ _____ _____ (what does it do?)

Living in the sea.

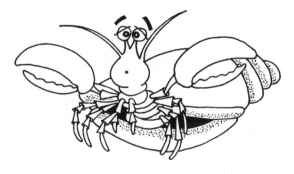

ASSOCIATIVE THINKING

Associative thinking requires identifying similar attributes in two or more items, events, or groups.

STEPS:

1. Identify basic attributes of the first items, event, or group

2. Identify basic attributes of additional items, events or groups

3. Identify those attributes similar to both items, events or groups

---

ORAL PRACTICE

1. A hippopotamus is like an elephant because…

2. A hot air balloon is like an airplane because…

3. A bathtub is like an ocean because…

4. A window is like a picture because…

5. A tooth is like a knife because…

BOOKTALKS : FROGS & TOADS

Days with Frog and Toad by Arnold Lobel. Harper & Row, 1979.

Frog and Toad are best friends. Toad is sometimes lazy as his messy house shows. There are clothes on the floor, dust on the chairs, windows that need washing, and plants that need watering. Toad does not want to get out of bed. He says he will do the work "tomorrow." But then Toad thinks that if he did the work today, he would have all day tomorrow to do what he likes to do best…sleep! In other stories, Frog helps Toad to fly a kite, Frog reads Toad a scary story, and Frog gives Toad a hat for his birthday that is too big. No matter what the problem, Frog and Toad are always together as good friends.

Froggy Plays T-Ball by Jonathan London. Illus. by Frank Remkiewicz. Viking, 2007.

It's Froggy's first day on the T-ball team, and he couldn't be more excited. His dad is the coach and his whole family is cheering him on. But when Coach Dad tells him to catch some flies out in right field, he takes the advice and catches some real flies (the kind that fly around with wings). Froggy can't seem to do anything right, but once he starts paying attention, his playing improves. He even hits a home run, and runs all the way…to his house! Here is another fun book in the "Froggy" series that includes *Froggy Gets Dressed* and *Froggy Rides a Bike*.

GO-TOGETHER WORDS

Find two words that go together and tell why.

Froggy	**day**	**team**	**dad**
coach	**T-ball**	**flies**	**field**
family	**advice**	**gusto**	**home**
run	**play**	**cheer**	**shirt**
head	**house**	**hits**	**catch**

FROG RIDDLES

Think of words that rhyme with frog.

    bog   dog   log   flog   hog   jog

What does the word mean? Log: wood cut from a tree.

Ask a question using the meaning of the word.

    Example: What would you call a frog lumberjack?

    Answer: A Log Frog

More Riddles:

What would you call a frog that says bow-wow?

    (dog frog)

What would you call a frog that lives in a swamp?

    (bog frog)

What would you call a frog that runs every morning?

    (jog frog)

What other riddles can you make?

Think of words that rhyme with TOAD.

Write toad riddles.

ATTRIBUTE LISTING

Attribute listing is the process of analyzing and separating data by observing and identifying a variety of qualities about a particular object, character, topic, or problem.

STEPS:

1. Select and state the object to be examined.

2. List the physical qualities and attributes.

3. List the social qualities or attributes.

4. List other objects or situations having many of the same qualities or attributes.

5. Combine attributes of different objects creating a new object, product or solution.

ORAL PRACTICE

Choose an animal.

What physical characteristics do you notice about the animal? (Physical attributes)

Would the animal be a good pet? (Social attributes)

Name another animal that would be a good pet for the same reasons.

What parts of two or more animals can be combined to make a perfect pet?

BOOKTALKS : PUMPKINS

Too Many Pumpkins by Linda Arms White. Illus. by Megan Lloyd. Holiday House, 1996.

An old woman had a great dislike for pumpkins so imagine her surprise when a pumpkin landed in her yard and scattered its seeds. Before long she had a whole yard full of pumpkins. First, she ignored them. She would not look at them. The pumpkins kept growing. There were far too many to pick and cart away. Whatever was she to do? She would make pumpkin treats, light up the path to her house with jack-o-lanterns, and invite the whole town to enjoy the treats. Can you guess all the treats she made?

Pumpkin Hill by Elizabeth Spurr. Illus. by Whitney Martin. Holiday House, 2006.

One small pumpkin grew on a hill. It grew and grew and grew until one day it left its vine and rolled away. It hit a stone and scattered its seeds all over the hill. No one notices when the seeds begin to sprout. No one notices when pumpkins grow all over the hill. The pumpkins get bigger and bigger. They break from their vines and roll down the hill right into the town…the streets were filled with thousands of pumpkins. The mayor called a meeting of all of the citizens. What could they do with thousands of pumpkins? The children carved six thousand jack-o-lanterns and carried them on Halloween. Mothers made three thousand and five pumpkin pies.

When the hill was entirely clear of pumpkins it made a great place for winter sledding. Pumpkin seeds, of course, were never again allowed in the town.

A PUMPKIN CHANT

List words to describe pumpkins

_____ pumpkins

_____ pumpkins

_____ pumpkins

_____ pumpkins

Lots of pumpkins, lots of pumpkins, all in a row.

List uses for a pumpkin

Pumpkin _____

Pumpkin _____

Pumpkin _____

Pumpkin _____

In a patch, on a hill, watch the pumpkins grow!

Read the pumpkin chant.

PUMPKINS AND APPLES: DIFFERENT AND ALIKE

Sing to the tune of "Mary Had a Little Lamb."

Mr. Lumpkin picked a pumpkin

Picked a pumpkin, picked a pumpkin

Mr. Lumpkin picked a pumpkin

Picked it off a vine

Mrs. Dapple picked an apple

Picked an apple, picked an apple

Mrs. Dapple picked an apple

Inside she found _____

Mrs. Dapple picked an apple

Picked an apple, picked an apple

Mrs. Dapple picked an apple

Picked it off a tree

Mr. Lumpkin picked a pumpkin

Picked a pumpkin, picked a pumpkin

Mr. Lumpkin picked a pumpkin

Made a pumpkin _____

Mr. Lumpkin picked a pumpkin

Picked a pumpkin, picked a pumpkin

Mr. Lumpkin picked a pumpkin

Inside he found _____

Mrs. Dapple picked an apple

Picked an apple, picked an apple

Mrs. Dapple picked an apple

Made an apple _____

Missing words: seeds, pie

BRAINSTORM

To **brainstorm** is to elicit many responses to a question or problem without evaluating each response. Quantity of responses is encouraged and all responses are accepted.

STEPS:

1. State a specific problem or ask an open-ended question.

2. State the rules for brainstorming:

   Accept all ideas, no criticism.

   Include unusual and creative ideas.

   Encourage "hitchhiking" on each other's ideas.

3. At the conclusion of the brainstorming session, comment on the number and variety of responses.

ORAL PRACTICE

1. How many ways can you serve potatoes?

2. How many excuses can you give for being late to school?

3. Name wild things you would see if you took a walk through the woods.

4. How many foods can you name that begin with the letter C?

BOOKTALKS : FOOD

The Wolf's Chicken Stew by Keiko Kasza. Putnam, 1987.

A hungry wolf spies a chicken and decides to fatten her up for a delicious chicken stew. Each morning he leaves good things to eat at her door: one hundred delicious pancakes, one hundred scrumptious doughnuts, and a cake that weighs one hundred pounds. When he decides she is plump enough he makes his way to her cottage and knocks on her door. He is greeted with thanks as the baby chicks give him one hundred kisses. The wolf's plan for chicken stew disappears and he heads home to "bake the little critters one hundred scrumptious cookies."

One Potato, Two Potato by Cynthia DeFelice. Illus. by Andrea U'Ren. Farrar, Straus & Giroux, 2006.

Imagine a husband and wife so poor that they had to share everything. They share one chair, one blanket and one potato. Also they each have one wish. Each wants to have one friend. One day they dug the last potato from the ground and discovered a big black pot. It was a magic pot. Whatever went into the pot came out as two. Soon, they had two potatoes, two blankets, and two chairs. Then came the day that the wife tripped and fell into the pot and her husband fell in as well. Out came two wives and two husbands. Now that they had the friend they wished for, they buried the pot for others to find.

HELPING FARMER BROWN

Every night Foxy Loxy sneaks into the hen house and takes one of Farmer Brown's chickens. Soon all the chickens will be gone.

Soon Farmer Brown won't have eggs to sell.

Soon Mrs. Farmer Brown won't have eggs to cook for breakfast.

Brainstorm ways the chickens can keep Foxy Loxy away from the hen house.

Brainstorm ways Farmer Brown can keep Foxy Loxy out of the hen house.

Brainstorm safe places Farmer Brown could keep the chickens other than the hen house.

Brainstorm things Farmer Brown could sell other than eggs.

Brainstorm all the foods Mrs. Farmer Brown can fix for breakfast other than eggs.

VEGETABLES

Suppose a cook made a vegetable stew rather than a chicken stew. Brainstorm names of these vegetables.

1. Vegetables that begin with the letter C.

2. Names of vegetables that have two or more syllables.

3. Vegetables that are the color green.

4. Vegetable names that rhyme.

5. Vegetables that grow above the ground.

6. Vegetables that grow below the ground.

7. Vegetables that come in cans.

8. Vegetables whose names begin with the same letter as the first name of each member of the group or class.

CLASSIFICATION

To **classify** is to identify or arrange objects or ideas according to a common characteristic or a unifying relationship. The group of objects or ideas would then have a common label.

STEPS:

1. Select a basis for grouping.

2. Examine each item to identify its characteristics or features.

3. Identify similarities and differences.

4. Place items with common features in the same category or group.

ORAL PRACTICE

Name as many animal pets as you can.

What pets can be grouped by their covering?

(fur, feathers, scales)

What pets could be grouped by their number of legs?

(two legs, four legs, no legs)

What pets could be grouped by the way they move?

(walk, fly, swim)

What other groups can we think of for animal pets?

BOOKTALKS : PETS

Pet Show! by Ezra Jack Keats. Viking, 1972.

On the day of the pet show, Archie could not find his cat. There was a prize for every pet, "the handsomest frog, the friendliest fish, the longest dog and the fastest mouse." When Archie brought a pet in a jar he said it was a germ. It won a ribbon for the quietest pet. Then an old woman arrived with a cat. It won a ribbon as the cat with the longest whiskers. It was Archie's cat. Archie was so happy to have his pet back that he told the woman to keep the ribbon. "It looks good on you," he said. "See you around."

Peanut by Linas Alsenas. Scholastic, 2007.

Mildred was a very lonely senior citizen until she finds a most unusual stray puppy. This puppy is rather large. He doesn't roll over. He never fetches and his nose is much bigger than any puppy she has ever seen. He would not eat dog food or chew on bones. The only thing he liked were peanuts so she named him Peanuts. In her apartment he watered her plants with his long nose. He squashed cereal boxes. One day when Mildred was taking Peanuts for a walk, a man from the circus ran up to Peanuts. The missing elephant had been found. Mildred visited Peanuts at the circus and knew he was happiest there. She went looking for another pet…a kitten, and decided to take it home. (The kitten was really a camel.)

GROUPING PETS

Cut apart these pictures and put them in groups. Give the name
  of each group.

SENTENCES

The pets who won prizes in Archie's pet show were:

A parrot	A frog	A fish	A canary	An ant
A goldfish	A dog	A mouse	A puppy	A cat

Complete these sentences by finding two pets alike and one different.

Example:

A goldfish has scales. A goldfish can swim.

A fish has scales. A fish can swim.

A parrot does not have scales A parrot cannot swim.

A _____ has _____.

A _____ has _____.

A _____ does not have _____.

A _____ can _____.

A _____ can _____.

A _____ cannot _____.

COMPARING

In **comparing** two objects or situations, similarities and differences are observed and identified.

STEPS:

1. Select a basis for comparison. (size, shape, uses, order, behavior)

2. Describe the features or characteristics to be compared.

3. Describe similarities and differences.

4. Summarize major similarities and differences.

ORAL PRACTICE

1. How is a chair like a table?

2. How is a chair different from a table?

3. How is a dog like a cat?

4. How is a dog different from a cat?

5. How is an apartment like a house?

6. How is an apartment different from a house?

BOOKTALKS : FEELINGS

Alert! by Etienne Delessert. Houghton Mifflin, 2007.

Tobias, the mole, collects shiny round pebbles and hides them in the tunnels to his burrow to keep them safe from robbers. When a friend tells Tobias that there are robbers on the prowl, he begins to worry about the safety of his pebbles. Should he scatter the pebbles throughout the tunnels or keep them together in one room where he can guard them? Day after day he becomes more worried and afraid. He moves his pebbles from one place to another until he discovers that he has been tricked into letting his fears get the better of him.

Grumpy Gloria by Anna Dewdney. Viking, 2006.

Do pets have bad days? Do pets show their feelings? What happens when a pet's best friend gets another friend? Gloria, the bulldog, feels left out when a little girl, her best friend, plays with other friends. The children set about to make grumpy Gloria happy again. They give her a doggie chew, brush her hair, take her jogging, give her a bath, a toy, and a bone. Gloria only gets grumpier. Nothing works until a spill from a bicycle finds Gloria with her best friend's arms around her.

I Love You Little Monkey by Alan Durant. Illus. by Katherine McEwen. Simon & Schuster, 2007.

Little Monkey wants to play but Big Monkey has too many chores to do. Little Monkey decides to help Big Monkey. Little Monkey proves not to be helpful at all. Rather than collecting figs for dinner, Little Monkey uses the figs for play; he messes up the bed and can't be quiet when Big Monkey wants to nap. No matter what mischief Little Monkey gets into, Big Monkey may not like the antics, but he never stops loving Little Monkey.

WHAT CAN YOU DO WITH PEBBLES?

Think of many things you can and cannot do with ten shiny pebbles.

What can you do with ten shiny pebbles?

You can _____

You can _____

You can _____

That's what you can do with ten shiny pebbles.

What can't you do with ten shiny pebbles?

You can't _____

You can't _____

You can't _____

No, you can't do that with ten shiny pebbles.

COMPARING ANIMALS

Use these words:

larger smaller longer shorter fatter faster slower taller

1. An elephant is _____ than a mole.

2. A mouse is _____ than a mole.

3. A giraffe is _____ than an elephant.

4. A pig is _____ than a cat.

5. A giraffe's neck is _____ than a horse's neck.

6. A pig's tail is _____ than a horse's tail.

7. A turtle moves _____ than a mouse.

8. A deer runs _____ than a pig.

Answer Key: 1. larger 2. smaller 3. taller 4. fatter 5. longer 6. shorter 7. slower 8. faster

COMPREHENSION

Comprehension requires establishing relationships among ideas which are then summarized and interpreted.

Steps:

1. Remember, recall, or read information from a story or on a topic.

2. Relate the information to previous knowledge.

3. Explain and/or summarize information.

4. Interpret the relationship between information and previous knowledge.

5. Encode the information in a new format.

ORAL PRACTICE

1. How many words can we use to describe Curious George?

2. What is the best word to describe Curious George other than the word, curious?

3. After sharing a story, ask these comprehension questions:

   A. Who did you like best in the story? Why?

   B. Was there a character you did not like in the story? Why?

   C. Give three words to describe a character in the story. Why did you choose these three words?

BOOKTALKS : CATS

Millions of Cats by Wanda Gag. (Reissue) Putnam's, 1996.

One day a little old man sets out to find a cat for his wife. He walked a very long time over hills and through valleys until he came to a hill that was covered with millions of cats. There were so many cats that the old man could not choose just one to take home…so he chose them all. On the way home the millions of cats drank all the water in a pond and ate all the grass from a hillside. The little old woman was dismayed to see her husband arrive with millions of cats. "We can't feed them all," she said. "Let the cats decide which is the prettiest. That is the one we will keep." As you can imagine, the cats fought and fought until they ate each other up. Only one ugly little cat was left who did not fight. He because the couple's most cherished pet.

The Cat Who Wouldn't Come Inside by Cynthia von Buhler. Houghton Mifflin, 2006.

On a cold winter day a lady sees a cat outside with snow on its back. She invites the cat inside but the cat runs away. Day after day the cat returns and takes each of the good things she leaves on her porch. Day one the woman leaves warm milk and each day she adds something else a cat would like: tuna, a catnip mouse, a soft rug, a cozy armchair, a ball of yarn, curtains, and a warm fire. Each time the cat refuses to come inside until at last the porch is so cozy that the cat makes it her home.

STORIES AND RHYMES

Read the Mother Goose Rhyme and the booktalk.

How many ways are the rhyme and the story alike?

The Kilkenny Cats

There once were two cats of Kilkenny.

Each thought there was one cat too many;

So they fought and they fit,

And they scratched and they bit,

Till, excepting their nails,

And the tips of their tails,

Instead of two cats, there weren't any.

The Little Old Woman and the Hungry Cat by Nancy Polette. Illus. by Frank Modell. Greenwillow Books, 1991.

One morning a little old woman baked cupcakes and told her cat to leave them alone while she went to the mayor's house with her sewing basket. The cat gobbled down the cupcakes, then went for a walk where he met and swallowed down a one-legged man and his squealing pig, a groom, a bride, a best man, a maid of honor, and four horses. When the little old woman came home, the cat swallowed her, sewing basket and all. She used her scissors to cut a hole in the cat's side big enough for all to step out.

Instead of attending the wedding party, the cat had to spend the whole day sewing up the hole in his side.

MILLIONS OF CATS

Add the missing words. Sing the song to the tune of "Mary Had A Little Lamb." Some words will be used more than once.

fight   kitten   cat   one   hills   wife   cats   pet

A husband went to find a (1) _____

Find a (2) _____

Find a (3) _____

A husband went to find a (4) _____

And found a million (5) _____

His wife said "We must choose just (6) _____

Choose just (7) _____

Choose just (8) _____

His wife said "We must choose just (9) _____

That one will be our (10) _____

The cats got into a big (11) _____

A big (12) _____

A big (13) _____

The cats got into a big (14) _____

And ate each other up.

Left by the door was one small (15) _____

One small (16) _____

One small (17) _____

Left by the door was one small (18) _____

And it became their (19) _____

Answer Key: 1, 2, 3, 4. kitten 5. cats 6, 7, 8, 9. one 10. pet 11, 12, 13, 14. fight 15, 16, 17, 18. cat 19. pet

DECISION MAKING

Decision making is the process leading to the selection of one of several options after consideration of facts, ideas, possible alternatives, probable consequences, and personal values.

Steps:

1. Identify the problem.

2. List alternative solutions.

3. Establish criteria for weighing each alternative.

   Example: 1 = no 2 = maybe 3 = yes

4. Choose the alternative with the highest rating.

5. Give reasons for your choice.

ORAL PRACTICE

Listing Alternatives

Problem: You are hungry.

1. Name three foods healthier to eat than pizza.

   Which food should you choose to eat?

Problem: You must cross a busy street to get home.

2. Name three ways to cross a street safely.

   Which way is best?

3. Name three reasons NOT to swim alone in a pond.

   Which reason is best?

BOOKTALKS : FOOD

Cloudy With A Chance of Meatballs by Judy Barrett. Illus. by Ron Barrett. Aladdin Books, 1978.

There were no supermarkets in the town of Chewandswallow since breakfast, lunch, and dinner fell from the sky. Breakfast began with a shower of orange juice followed by low clouds of sunny-side up eggs and toast. Lunch might be frankfurters already in their rolls followed by mustard clouds. People listened to the weather report to find out what they would be eating the next day.

It was quite a nice arrangement until one day the weather took a turn for the worse. The food that fell from the sky got larger and larger and so did the portions. The residents of Chewandswallow feared for their lives and had to escape. They floated on large slices of stale bread for a week until they reached a town that welcomed them. This is the tall tale Grandfather loves to tell.

Pancakes for Supper! by Anne Isaacs. Illus. by Mark Teague. Scholastic, 2006.

Toby is all dressed up and on her way to town when she falls out of the wagon and lands in a deep, dark forest. She meets five wild animals but trades them a piece of her clothing for her safety. The animals argued about which was the grandest and ran around and around the maple tree so fast that they turned into a golden brown puddle. Toby and her parents found each other and under the warm sun the tree soaked up the puddle. Toby got a bucket and caught the sweet maple syrup that trickled down. "Pancakes for supper!" she shouted.

BREAKFAST

Suppose you got up late and needed a good breakfast to give you energy during the day. You will have to hurry so you won't be late for school.

Score each breakfast 1 = no 2 = maybe 3 = yes

The first food is scored for you.

Breakfast	Easy to make	Fast	Good for Energy	Total
Eggs	2	1	2	5
Cereal				
Pancakes				
Toast				

The best breakfast is _____

_____

THE BEST SNACK

Sometimes having too much food to choose from is not a good thing. Some foods are healthier to eat than others.

What would be the best thing to bring for a snack at school?

Score each item 1 = no 2 = maybe 3 = yes

The first item is scored for you.

Food	Easy to make & take	Good for you	Tastes good	Total
Popcorn	2	3	3	8
Cupcakes				
Ice Cream				
Apple				

DEDUCTIVE THINKING

Deductive thinking is the ability to arrive at one correct answer after examining several clues. Delaying judgment until all clues have been examined is essential.

Steps:

1. Examine the question to be answered.

2. Carefully examine and reflect on the data (clues) available.

3. Identify relationships among clues.

4. Arrive at a conclusion supported by the data.

ORAL PRACTICE

Where does this story take place?

It does not take place in the city.

It does not take place on the ocean.

It does not take place in the jungle.

The animals in this story hide behind trees.

The story must take place in the _____

BOOKTALKS : ANIMAL FRIENDS

My Friend Rabbit by Eric Rohmann. Roaring Brook Press, 2002.

When Mouse lets his best friend, Rabbit, play with his brand new airplane, trouble isn't far behind. Rabbit means well but he is much bigger than Mouse and when he tried to launch the plane it ends up in a tree, too high to reach. Rabbit tells Mouse not to worry since he has an idea. Rabbit gathers together lots of animals and gets them to climb on each other. A tall tree of animals results with rhino on top of elephant, hippo on top of rhino, antelope on top of hippo, crocodile on top of antelope, bear on top of crocodile, goose on top of bear, and squirrel on top of goose holding mouse. Reaching for the plane proves to be a disaster when the animal ladder collapses sending the animals bouncing every which way. Mouse is left hanging on to the wing of the plane which is still stuck in the tree. Finally the plane is rescued but trouble looms again when Rabbit tries to take a plane ride with Mouse.

Where Is Bear? By Lesléa Newman. Illus. by Valeri Gorbachev. Harcourt, 2004.

The forest animals begin a game of hide and seek. While Bunny counts to ten, Fox and Frog hide behind a log. Turtle hides in his shell. Chipmunk, Skunk, Snake, Ant, Beetle, and Ladybug all find places to hide. So does Bear. When Rabbit finishes counting he finds all of the hidden animals except Bear. The animals join in the search. They look behind rocks and trees, along the creek and in the woods, but no Bear. Last they look in a deep, dark cave. Sure enough they find Bear sound asleep. They wake Bear up with a kiss but Bear can't stay awake long enough to play the game again.

MYSTERY ANIMALS

Listen to the clues one at a time. Guess the mystery animal.

1. **Clues**
   A. I live in the forest.
   B. I have four legs.
   C. I have a long tail.
   D. My name rhymes with BOX.

2. **Clues**
   A. I live in the forest
   B. I have four legs.
   C. I sleep through the winter.
   D. My name rhymes with CARE.

3. **Clues**
   A. I live in the forest.
   B. I have four legs.
   C. I am black and white.
   D. My name rhymes with SHRUNK.

Write your own animal riddles for others to guess.

Answer Key: 1. fox 2. bear 3. skunk

FOREST SOUNDS

Skunk, Rabbit, Turtle, and Snake heard different sounds while playing hide and seek. Which animal heard which sound?

CLUES

1.   Skunk hid by a small stream.

2.   Turtle heard a sound that begins with the first letter of his name.

3.   Snake hid in a bird's nest.

4.   Rabbit hid in a dark cave.

SOUND ANIMAL

A. Water rippling _____

B. Bear snoring _____

C. Trees swaying _____

D. Wings flapping _____

Answer Key: Skunk: water rippling; Turtle: trees swaying; Rabbit: bear snoring; Snake: wings flapping

ELABORATION

Elaboration is the process of adding details to an existing product.

Steps:

1. Examine the basic object or idea to be changed or improved by elaboration.

2. Define the basic idea.

3. Decide how to add or expand on the basic idea to make it more interesting or complete.

4. Add details to develop a more interesting or useful product or idea.

ORAL PRACTICE

1. What could you add to your classroom to make it easy to get out during a fire drill?

2. What could you add to your pencil to make it easier to do homework?

3. If you added an eye to the end of your finger, what could you do that you cannot do now?

4. What could you add to Humpty Dumpty so that he would not break into pieces if he fell off a wall?

BOOKTALKS : SOMETHING ADDED

Miss Nelson is Missing! by Harry Allard. Illus. by James Marshall. Houghton Mifflin, 1977.

The kids in Room 207 were about the worst kids in the school. They threw spitballs, were rude during story hour, and never did their homework. Their teacher, Miss Nelson, was a very kind person but even kind people don't like being taken advantage of. She stopped coming to school and her replacement was the dreaded Miss Viola Swamp. No one misbehaved in Miss Swamp's class. Everyone did homework. Not a spitball was thrown and there was NO story hour. The children went to the police for help in finding Miss Nelson but the police couldn't help. They were just about to give up hope when Miss Nelson returned. She discovered that her students had changed for the better and smiled to herself as she put away Miss Viola Swamp's clothes in her closet that night.

Imogene's Antlers by David Small. Crown Publishers, 1985.

Suppose you woke up one morning to discover you had acquired part of an animal! This is what happens to Imogene when she awakens to find she has sprouted antlers. They do cause SOME difficulty for her in getting dressed and going through doors. Her mother faints at the sight of Imogene with antlers. None of the experts consulted could help Imogene but she did discover that antlers have some useful purposes. They are an excellent place to hang and dry towels. They make an outstanding bird feeder. But Imogene doesn't really want to be a towel rack or a bird feeder. How Imogene's problem is solved makes for funny reading.

SAVE THE WORM

Imogene's antlers made an excellent bird feeder. Suppose she loses her antlers and the birds go looking for worms. What can you add to this picture to save the worm from becoming the bird's breakfast?

MISS NELSON'S HAT

What can you add to Miss Nelson's new hat so that everyone will notice it?

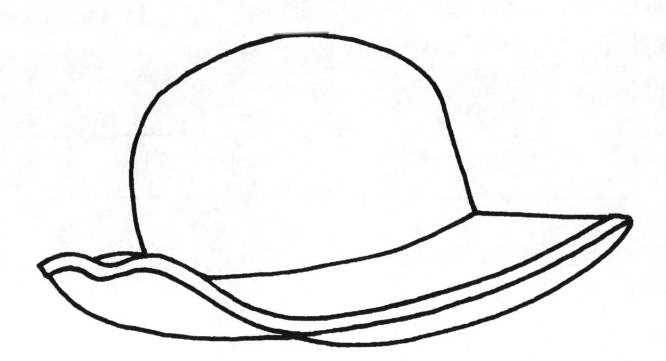

EVALUATION

Evaluation requires the weighing of positive and negative factors in choosing the best plan of action.

Steps:

1. Identify what is to be evaluated.

2. Define the standards of appraisal.

3. Collect data related to the defined standards.

4. Collect an equal number of positive and negative points to avoid prejudice.

5. Make a judgment.

ORAL PRACTICE

Share: *Horton Hatches the Egg* by Dr. Seuss. Random House, 1940.
Horton, the elephant, agrees to sit on lazy Mayzie's egg while she takes a vacation. She does not return all through the fall, winter and spring. Hunters capture Horton and put him on display in a circus. Just as the egg is about to hatch Mayzie shows up. She wants her egg back.

Give an equal number of reasons why Horton should get the egg and why Mayzie should get the egg. After examining all of the reasons for and against, vote on who should get the egg.

Finish the story to discover the decision that the author (Dr. Seuss) made.

BOOKTALKS : SCHOOL STORIES

Hooway for Wodney Wat by Helen Lester. Illus. by Lynn Munsinger. Houghton Mifflin, 1999.

Wodney Wat had a problem. He could not pronounce words that began with or contained the letter, R. Wodney's friends don't seem to mind. The rodents in Miss Fuzzleworth's class got along fine until the day Camilla Capybara showed up. She bragged that she was bigger, meaner, and smarter than anyone in the class. The small rodents trembled in fright.

For afternoon recess Wodney is chosen to be the leader of "Simon Says." His directions to "weed the sign, wake the leaves and go west" are easily understood by his classmates. Camilla, however, tries to pull up weeds, wake up the leaves, and finally head west never to be seen again. Wodney Wat saves the day and becomes a hero.

Chrysanthemum by Kevin Henkes. Greenwillow Books, 1991.

Because her parents thought she was an absolutely perfect baby they gave her a very special name. Chrysanthemum. Chrysanthemum loved her name especially when mother used it to wake her up or father used it to call her to dinner. But going to school for the first time was a shock. The other children made fun of her name. They said it was too long and would not fit on her name tag. They said she was a flower to be picked and smelled. Each day Chrysanthemum took longer and longer to get to school. When she was chosen to be a daisy in the school musical the children laughed again. But the music teacher saw nothing funny about being named for a flower since her name was Delphinium. When the girls heard this, they all wanted flower names as well. Chrysanthemum bloomed!

WHAT WOULD YOU DO?

Wodney Wat was very shy and bashful. The teacher wants him to lead the game of "Simon Says." Give reasons Wodney should say yes and reasons he should say no.

There is a bully in your school who takes things, and hits other children. Give reasons to ignore the bully and reasons to try to make friends with the bully.

Give reasons you would like to be a bully and reasons you would not like to be a bully.

Your parents want to name your new baby sister after a flower. Give reasons why this is a good idea and reasons why it is not a good idea.

The children are teasing a child in your class about his or her unusual name. Give reasons to join in the teasing and reasons not to join in the teasing.

CHOICES

Tell which you would rather have and why.

new clothes new name new school new shoes _____ _____ _____	a rose a petunia a violet a tulip _____ _____ _____
a dragon a hamster a pony a monkey _____ _____ _____	a good friend a lot of money a big house a kind teacher _____ _____ _____

FLEXIBILITY

Flexibility is the ability to respond in a variety of categories, to find new uses for familiar objects or new ways of dealing with familiar situations. Flexibility requires thinking beyond the usual and obvious to the new and original.

Steps:

1. Identify the information to be used.

2. Examine the items to be used.

3. Identify many categories for the material.

4. Respond with new and creative categories or uses.

ORAL PRACTICE

Why Did the Chicken Cross the Road? Illus. by fourteen artists. Dial 2006.

Fourteen different artists answer the question, "Why did the chicken cross the road?" Tedd Arnold said, "To show the possum it could be done." David Shannon said, "The chicken crossed the road because the light was green."

How many funny reasons can you give to answer the question: Why did the chicken cross the road?

BOOKTALKS : CHANGING PLACES

Mike Mulligan and His Steam Shovel by Virginia Lee Burton. Houghton Mifflin, 1967.

Mike Mulligan and his steam shovel, Mary Anne, had worked together for many years. They dug canals, tunnels, and roadways. Mike bragged that Mary Anne could dig as much in a day as one hundred men could dig in a week. The years pass and Mary Anne is no longer needed to dig canals and tunnels. Mike has to find a new place for her to dig. The two are put to the test and asked to dig a basement for the Town Hall. Mike and Mary Anne are so busy digging that they forget to plan how to get out of the large hole. Then a young boy thinks of a perfect solution. Mary Anne will be needed in a new place for years to come!

What do you suppose the solution was?

The Little House by Virginia Lee Burton. Houghton Mifflin, 1942.

The little house sat on a hill in the countryside and was happy watching the changing seasons and the activities she saw with each. The farmer planted and harvested his crops. In the summer the children swam in the pond and in the fall they went to school. She liked watching the children on their sleds in the winter and seeing the apples trees bloom in the spring. But roads were built, machines came and soon houses, then tall buildings and a whole city grew up around her. She missed the daisies and the apple trees and seeing the children at play. She was forgotten until one day a lady saw her. The lady had played in the house as a child. She bought the house and had it moved to the country where once again the little house could watch the seasons come and go.

WHY DO WE DIG HOLES?

How many reasons can you give to dig a hole in the ground? Write your ideas on the lines in this poem.

        Steam shovel, steam shovel, dig all day

        Steam shovel, steam shovel, dig away

Dig a hole to _____

Dig a hole to _____

        Steam shovel, steam shovel, dig all day

        Steam shovel, steam shovel, dig away

        Steam shovel, steam shovel, dig all day

Dig a hole to _____

Dig a hole to _____

        Steam shovel, steam shovel, dig all day

        Steam shovel, steam shovel, dig away

CITY LIFE

A little house was unhappy when tall city buildings and busy, noisy streets were built all around it.

Help the little house feel better by completing these sentences.

1. Seeing tall buildings all around you is bad, but seeing

    _____

    all around you is worse.

2. Hearing noisy cars go by all day is bad, but hearing

    _____

    go by is worse.

3. Smelling garbage trucks all day is bad, but smelling

    _____

    all day is worse.

4. Being lost in a crowd of people is bad, but

    _____ in a

    crowd of people is worse.

FLUENCY

Fluency is the ability to produce common responses to a given situation. The emphasis is on quantity rather than quality. The intent is to build a large store of information or material for further selective use.

Steps:

1. Define the situation and determine the category.

2. Ask for many responses.

3. Do not allow evaluation of responses.

4. Accept all ideas given.

ORAL PRACTICE

1. Name all the jobs that need to be done on a farm.

2. Name many signs of fall.

3. Name all the things children can do for fun in the winter.

4. Name many forms of transportation used today to buy and sell.

5. Make a list of all the things class members could make to take to town to trade or sell.

BOOKTALKS : LIFE ON THE FARM

The Ox-cart Man by Barbara Cooney. Viking Press, 1979.

A farmer in New Hampshire loaded his cart with all the products he and his family made or grew during the past year that they did not use themselves. The farmer's ox-cart was loaded with wool, a shawl, mittens, candles, linen, shingles, brooms, potatoes, apples, cabbages, and other products of this farm family's labors. The farmer was ready to travel to Portsmouth to trade and sell. After a ten day journey, he arrived at the market where he sold everything including the ox cart, yoke, harness, and ox. The farmer then bought an iron kettle, an embroidery needle, a whittling knife and wintergreen candies. He then returned home to his family with gifts and a pocketful of coins. Once again, the ox-cart man and his family repeated the seasonal cycle, preparing for the next trading trip to town.

From Dawn till Dusk by Natalie Kinsey-Warnock. Illus. by Mary Azarian. Houghton Mifflin, 2002.

A farmer's family has work to do all year around but there are many fun times as well. The children gathered by a warm fire and listened to stories on cold winter nights. They made maple sugar-on-snow, dug tunnels, made snow forts, and had snowball fights. In the spring they made mud pies and splashed through puddles. They dug worms and went fishing. Summer was time for swimming in the pond, welcoming new kittens, and plates and plates of fresh vegetables. Fall was harvest time, climbing apple trees to shake the apples down, and, of course, time for school. As the seasons repeat themselves year after year, the children are sure they would not want to live anywhere else.

HOW MANY ANSWERS?

How many answers can you give?

1. The branches of an apple tree are like…

2. A wool shirt is as scratchy as…

3. Feathers remind me of…

4. Mittens could be used for…

5. You can put honey on…

6. At night, light can come from…

7. A farmer can travel to town in/on a…

8. A shawl could be used to…

9. Other uses for a big bag of potatoes are…

10. Uses for an apple other than to eat are…

FOR SALE! FOR SALE!

Here are things a farmer might take to town to sell. Add a describing word to each and read the chant.

For Sale! For Sale!

_____ wool

_____ shawl

_____ candles

_____ brooms

All for sale, all for sale

And mittens to keep you warm.

_____ apples

_____ pumpkins

_____ cabbages

_____ turnips

All for sale, all for sale

All come from the farm.

FORECASTING

Forecasting requires looking at both the causes and effects of an action before determining the best action to take.

Steps:

1. Consider all possible causes of a given situation.

2. Consider all possible effects of a given situation.

3. Choose the best cause and effect.

4. Determine appropriate action(s) based on the choice.

5. Give reasons for choosing the action.

ORAL PRACTICE

1. Think of reasons people do not want to get out of bed in the morning.

2. What would happen if these workers did not get out of bed?

   A. Fireman

   B. Nurse

   C. Policeman

   D. Farmer

   E. Teacher

BOOKTALKS : FAMILY LIFE

Bedtime for Frances by Russell Hoban. Illus. by Garth Williams. HarperCollins, 1960.

Frances, the badger, like many children, has problems at bedtime. She needs a glass of milk and many kisses before being tucked into bed with her teddy bear and doll but it is not yet time for sweet dreams. Up she pops to tell her parents that there is a tiger in her room, a giant in the corner, and a crack in the ceiling that is getting wider. But finally a different kind of bumping and thumping puts Frances to sleep. Can you guess what it is?

A Baby Sister for Frances by Russell Hoban. Illus. by Lillian Hoban. HarperCollins, 1964.

With Gloria, her new baby sister at home, no one seems to pay attention to Frances. Mother doesn't have time to wash her favorite dress or go shopping for raisins for her oatmeal. Frances decides that evening to run away. She takes her nickels and pennies, her favorite toys, and her special blanket and tells her parents that she has found the perfect place to run away to . . . under the dining room table. She listens as her parents talk about how they miss her songs. They talk about how Gloria will miss having a big sister to teach her things. They mention how much they would like to hear from Frances so she calls them on a pretend telephone. She has decided to come home. Mother says that is a very good thing since she is making a chocolate cake and Gloria is too little to have some. And after all, one new baby doesn't make a family.

CAUSE AND EFFECT

Frances, the badger, took her book to bed each night. She took a flashlight, too. She hid under the covers and read her book.

One night her flashlight went out. She shook it and shook it but the light would not come on. She put her book away in a crack in the wall of her badger hole between two pieces of wood.

It rained all night long. In the morning, the book was so wet Frances could not turn the pages.

Answer these questions.

1. What caused Frances to read under the covers with a flashlight?

2. What caused the flashlight to go out?

3. What was the effect of not having a flashlight that worked?

4. What caused Frances to put the book away?

5. What was the effect of putting the book in a crack in the wall?

BOOKTALKS : ISLANDS AND SEASONS

The Little Island by Golden MacDonald. Illus. by Leonard Weisgard. Doubleday, 1946.

The little island lived alone in the ocean watching the changes the seasons brought to the plants and animals of the island. One day a kitten came to the island with some people on a picnic. The kitten thought the island was very little and must be very lonely. But the kitten discovered that the island was not separated from the rest of the world at all, but connected to the rest of the land under the water. The little island was content with its life as part of the world, yet, having a life of its own, surrounded by the bright blue sea.

Mouse's First Fall by Lauren Thompson. Illus. by Buket Erdogan. Simon & Schuster, 2006.

Mouse and his friend, Minka, go out to play on a cool fall day. They see leaves of all shapes and colors that have fallen from the trees. They run through the leaves and make a big pile of leaves. Minka jumps in the leaves and disappears. Mouse searches for her and out she jumps from the leaf pile. What fun on a beautiful fall day.

WHAT IS AN ISLAND?

What makes an island? What else can you call an island? What general statement can you make about islands?

Which of these is an island? Why?

SEASONS

What pictures can you draw that are true of each season?

Summer is...	**Fall is...**
Winter is...	**Spring is...**

HYPOTHESIZING

To **hypothesize** is to formulate a statement to support or deny with evidence showing how two or more items or situations are related.

Steps:

1. State and give reasons for the hypothesis.

2. Identify the needed data and procedures needed to test the hypothesis.

3. Conduct the data-gathering procedures.

4. Examine the data to see if the hypothesis is supported.

ORAL PRACTICE

Hypothesis: Most students in the class would rather read nonfiction than fiction.

Ask for a show of hands:

How many prefer to read nonfiction?

_____

How many prefer to read fiction?

_____

Most students prefer

_____

The hypothesis was _____ right _____ wrong

BOOKTALKS : WILD ANIMALS

Why Mosquitoes Buzz In People's Ears by Verna Aardema.
   Illus. by Leo and Diane Dillon. Dial Press, 1975.

One morning a mosquito tells an iguana a foolish tale that he doesn't want to hear. The iguana puts sticks in his ears and storms off. He passes a python and doesn't say good morning. The python thinks the iguana is mad at him, so he slithers down into a rabbit's den. This begins confusion throughout the jungle, which ends in the death of Mother Owl's owlet. Mother Owl, who is both angry and sad, refuses to wake the sun. When the animals who do not like the dark days, find out that mosquito is guilty, Mosquito has to pay for his foolishness. Mother Owl again wakes the sun.

Chameleon's Colors by Chisato Tashiro. North-South Books, 2007.

Chameleon is tired of constantly changing colors. He blends in wherever he goes and no one ever sees him! Hippo, however, is envious of Chameleon. He would love to be a different color. Surprisingly, all of the other animals of the jungle would, too. So, Chameleon sets to work painting stripes on the lion and polka-dots on the elephant. He uses every color and pattern under the sun. But, as the animals soon learn, changing their original appearance causes problems they never expected.

ABOUT MOSQUITOES

Hypothesis:

When mosquitoes buzz in people's ears, most people would slap at it.

Check your hypothesis by asking your classmates what they would do. Place a check mark under each heading for each answer you receive.

Go Inside	Buzz Back	Slap	Spray	Other

BUZZ POLL RESULTS

Most people:

_____ Go inside

_____ Buzz back

_____ Slap at the mosquito

_____ Spray bug spray

_____ Other

My hypothesis was: _____ Right _____ Wrong

ABOUT COLORS

Hypothesis:

The favorite color of boys is red. The favorite color of girls is blue.

Check your hypothesis by asking your classmates their favorite color. Place a check mark under each heading for each answer you receive.

B = Boys G = Girls

	Red	Yellow	Blue	Green	Other
B					
G					

COLOR POLL RESULTS

BOYS   **GIRLS**

_____ Red _____

_____ Yellow _____

_____ Blue _____

_____ Green _____

_____ Other _____

My hypothesis [for boys] was: _____ Right _____ Wrong

My hypothesis [for girls] was: _____ Right _____ Wrong

IMAGINATION

Without **imagination** nothing could ever be created by people.

> With imagination, we can:
>
> Invent new things
>
> Make pictures in the head
>
> Make up characters
>
> Look into the future

ORAL PRACTICE

What could you do if you had eyes in the back of your head?

What could you do if you had wings?

If you were twenty feet tall, what could you do that you cannot do now?

If you were granted three wishes, what would they be?

If your favorite book character visited your house, what new adventure would you ask him or her to have?

BOOKTALKS : MAGIC AND IMAGINATION

Where the Wild Things Are by Maurice Sendak. HarperCollins, 1963.

Max has misbehaved. He is sent to his room to think things over and his imaginative mind dreams up a river, a boat and a forest. He sails away to an imaginary kingdom where there are no parents to send you to your room. Max's room becomes a kingdom with tall trees and wild things. Max, as king of the wild things, orders the rumpus to begin and romps through the forest with the scary looking creatures. After the romp he returns to his room where supper might be waiting after all.

Sylvester and the Magic Pebble by William Steig. Simon & Schuster, 1969.

Sylvester Duncan, a donkey, collects pebbles. One day he finds an unusual pebble in the meadow. He is rubbing the pebble when it begins to rain. He wishes the rain to stop and it does. He realizes that the pebble is magic and will grant his every wish. He meets a lion in the meadow and wishes to become a stone. His wish is granted, but the pebble rolls away from the stone. When Sylvester does not come home, his frantic parents search everywhere for him but do not find him. In the spring, Mr. Duncan takes Mrs. Duncan on a picnic to cheer her up. She finds the pebble and lays it on the stone. Sylvester becomes himself again and has a happy reunion with his parents.

IMAGINATION SONG

Choose from these words to complete the song.

book   boat   head   blow   bed   things   trees

Tune: "Twinkle, Twinkle, Little Star"

Just imagine you could float

One a cozy, cozy b_____ (1)

See the forest, see it grow

Hear the wind, oh, hear it b_____ (2)

Dancing round and round in rings

Dancing with the wild, wild t_____ (3)

Would you believe what [your name] sees

A forest filled with lots of _____ (4)

You don't have to leave your _____ (5)

See the wild things in your _____ (6)

Open a page and take a look

You can travel in a _____ (7)

Answer Key: 1. boat 2. blow 3. things 4. trees 5. bed 6. head 7. book

USE YOUR IMAGINATION

1. What is the donkey's name?

2. Where did he get the car?

3. Where is he going?

4. Who will he meet on the way?

5. What will go wrong with his trip?

6. Who will help? How?

7. What will the donkey do with the car at the end of the trip?

INFERRING

Inferring means drawing a possible consequence, conclusion, or implication from a set of facts.

Steps:

1. Read carefully the available facts.

2. Note the question to be answered.

3. Determine those facts that fit the question.

4. Draw a conclusion or inference.

ORAL PRACTICE

1. How do you suppose that your teacher gets to school before the children arrive?

2. How would the school day be different if there were no school bells throughout the day?

3. Why do you think you should not run during a fire drill?

4. Why do you suppose the principal has a special office?

BOOKTALKS : FARM ANIMALS

Henny Penny by Vivian French. Illus. by Sophie Windham. Bloomsbury Books, 2006.

One morning Henny Penny was outside shaking her dust cloth when the dust made her sneeze so hard that an acorn fell from a tree right on to her head. "The sky is falling," she shrieked. "I must go and tell the king."

On her way to the palace she met friends who joined her, Cocky Locky, Ducky Lucky, Goosey Loosey, and Turkey Lurky. They stop by the den of Foxy Loxy and he invites them to dinner. Henny Penny sees bones, feathers, and only one plate on the table. She knows that she and her friends will BE Foxy Loxy's dinner. She must think fast. How can she get everyone home safely?

How did Henny Penny know that Foxy Loxy was going to eat her and her friends for dinner?

The King's Chorus by Linda Hayward. Illus. by Jennifer P. Goldfinger. Clarion Books, 2006.

As King of the Barnyard, Kadoodle struts his stuff and crows at all hours of the day and night. No one on the farm can get any sleep. The cows and hens are kept awake all night. Finally, Honketta, the goose tells Kadoodle a story about another king and his noble chorus. The roosters in her story are heard around the world because they all crow at the same time, when the "King's eye" appeared in the sky. Kadoodle is impressed with the story and decides to wait until morning to join the "King's" chorus.

Who or what is the "King's eye"?

WHAT HAPPENED?

If a rooster crowed all night and kept the farm animals awake, what might or might not happen on the farm?

Complete each verse with the missing word.

Choose from these words:

story   eggs   wagon   cow   food

1. The farmer, too tired to plow,

   Forgets to milk the _____.

2. His wife is in a bad mood

   And decides not to fix any _____.

3. The chickens asleep on their legs

   Forget to lay any _____.

4. The donkey whose hind legs are draggin'

   Refused to pull the farm _____.

5. Honketta in all her glory

   Decided to tell a _____.

   Answer Key: 1. cow 2. food 3. eggs 4. wagon 5. story

THE TREE

Draw things other than an acorn that might fall from the tree to scare Henny Penny.

INTERPRET

To **interpret** is to get the meaning from a source.

Steps:

1. Ask: What are the main ideas?

2. What are the supporting details?

3. What relationship do you find between _____ and
   _____?

4. Explain the main idea in a new way or in your own words.

ORAL PRACTICE

Read aloud:

Once there was a girl and her name was Mary
She had a garden that was most contrary
Now Mary was lazy and she would not plant a seed
So all that she grew was weed after weed.
No wonder the garden was so contrary
Looked after by a girl called lazy Mary.

1. What do you know about Mary's garden?

2. What do you know about Mary?

3. Why do you think the garden was full of weeds?

4. What is the main idea of this verse?

BOOKTALKS : MUSIC

Berlioz the Bear written and illustrated by Jan Brett. G.P. Putnam's Sons, 1991.

Suppose you were asked to play at a ball. Suppose you were asked to bring the entire orchestra. Suppose you had trouble getting to the ball. That is what happened to Berlioz. First, he heard a strange noise in his double bass. It didn't sound like music at all. Next, after all the players climbed in the wagon, the wheel got stuck in a hole. None of the musicians could pull the wagon out of the hole. The mule did not want to pull the wagon. The mule sat down. The players were not discouraged. They used the time to put on their tail coats and tune up their instruments. Other animals who saw the wagon wheel in the hole stopped to help. A rooster, a cat, a billy goat, a plow horse, and an ox pulled and pulled on a rope to get the mule up. The mule would not budge. Time is quickly passing. It is almost time for the ball. The dancers are ready but there is no music. Then a bee who was hiding in the double bass flies out. The bee stings the mule. The mule jumps up and begins to pull the wagon. The musicians make it just in time to play for the dancers at the ball.

Jake, the Philharmonic Dog by Karen LeFrak. Illus. by Marcin Baranski. Walker, 2006.

Jake, the dog, loves music and playing fetch. He goes to work with Richie, a stagehand for the Philharmonic orchestra. Jake "woofs" with the woodwinds and "ruffs" with the horns, but knows to be quiet when the whole orchestra plays. Jake proves he is truly a musician's dog when the conductor loses his baton. He cannot lead the orchestra! Then Jake becomes the star of the evening when he finds the baton and fetches it on stage.

GETTING TO THE BALL

Complete the last lines to this poem.

Choose from these words:

> ball   rear   horn   that   ditch   stung

The orchestra was ready
Ready one and all
They climbed in the wagon
To go to the (1) _____

They started their trip
Early in the morn
The drums and the fiddles
And the bear with a (2) _____

The wagon was so full
It began to sway and pitch
The wagon wheel turned
And slid into a (3) _____

They pushed and they pulled
But the mule just sat
The wagon would not move
And that was (4) _____

But help was near by,
Yes, help was near.
A bee flew down
And (5) _____ the mule on the (6) _____

Answer Key: 1. ball 2. horn 3. ditch 4. that 5. stung 6. rear

WHAT I'D LIKE TO BE

Choose from these words:

music   violin   conductor   stage

A musician is what I'd like to be

And this is what I'd do, you see

Practice many hours at home

Go on (1) _____ and find my seat (Where do you sit?)

Warm up my (2) _____ (What instrument?)

Follow the (3) _____ (Who leads the orchestra?)

Read the (4) _____ to know what notes to play.

Play my instrument

Fill the concert hall with music.

But before I can do all this I have to get out of bed in the morning.

Answer Key: 1. stage 2. violin 3. conductor 4. music

JUDGING

To **judge** is to make an informed evaluation based on standards.

Steps:

1. Decide what is to be judged.

2. List the standards that apply.

3. Gather evidence to the extent to which each standard is met.

4. Consider evidence and make a judgment.

ORAL PRACTICE

Should children be required to go to school

    A. All year round?

    B. Only six months of the year?

    C. Nine to ten months of the year?

Check off factors to consider. Mark A, B, or C.

Standards: The best amount of time to:

_____ learn to read, write and do math

_____ get to know the teacher

_____ be a part of a school sports team

_____ learn subjects other than reading and math

Apply the standards and make a judgment. _____

BOOKTALKS : BIRTHDAYS

A Letter to Amy by Ezra Jack Keats. Harper & Row, 1968.

Peter wrote a letter to Amy to invite her to his birthday party. He went outside to mail it but the wind blew it out of his hand. Peter chased the letter but couldn't catch it. It began to rain. Peter bumped into Amy but caught the letter and quickly put it in the mailbox. Amy ran off crying and Peter was afraid she would not come to his party. All the others who were coming were boys. On party day Amy did come and brought a talking parrot. Having Amy at the party was the best gift of all.

Happy Birthday, Jamela! by Niki Daly. Farrar, Straus & Giroux, 2006.

Jamela went shopping with her mother for birthday clothes and shoes. She wanted the sparkly princess shoes, but mother said they would not do for school. Mother bought strong, black shoes for Jamela. When Jamela got home she got out her beads and glittery bits. Mother was not happy with the glittery shoes but an artist who saw them asked Jamela to help her make more. They sold them at a market stand and made enough money to buy another pair of school shoes. On birthday party day there were new school shoes, but imagine Jamela's surprise when she opened a box with the princess shoes. It was a very happy birthday!

WOULD YOU RATIIER...

Would you rather . . .

Choose one item in each group. Circle your choice. State your standard for the choice.

1. Have an all boys' birthday party? Have an all girls' birthday party? Have a birthday party with both boys and girls?

    Standard (Why?)_____

    _____

2. Have sturdy school shoes? Have sparkly princess shoes? Not have to wear shoes at all?

    Standard (Why?)_____

    _____

3. Be given ten dollars? Find ten dollars? Earn ten dollars?

    Standard (Why?)_____

    _____

4. Do the dishes? Mop the floor? Take out the trash?

    Standard (Why?)_____

    _____

THE PRICE OF FAME

Share: *The Tortoise and the Hare Race Again* by Dan
   Bernstein. Illus. by Andrew Glass. Holiday House, 2006.

   Tortoise is very sorry he won the race with Hare. Now he has to
march in parades which means six hours of smiling. He is challenged to races by the young tortoises who want to beat the champion. He cannot go anywhere without being surrounded by
admirers. All Tortoise really wants is "sleeping long hours and
slurping juicy worms." When Hare challenges Tortoise to another
race, Tortoise was delighted. This time he would make sure that
Hare wins.

If Hare wins the race, will he be happy as the new Racing
   Champion of the forest?

Standards: (Write yes or no after each standard.)

   1.   Will enjoy being much admired by others. _____

   2.   Will enjoy marching six hours in parades. _____

   3.   Will like being frequently challenged to races. _____

   4.   Will like not having a lot of quiet time alone. _____

After looking at your answers to each standard, should Hare let
   Tortoise win the race or try to win it himself? Why?

KNOWLEDGE

Knowledge is the accumulated sum of facts acquired by a person.

IN KNOWLEDGE ACQUISITION, THE LEARNER:

1. Is attentive

2. Absorbs information

3. Remembers

4. Practices, drills, recites

5. Discovers information

6. Recognizes information that has been previously learned.

ORAL PRACTICE

Demonstrate your knowledge of ABC order.

1. Name the letter that comes after D.

2. Name the letter that comes before L.

3. Name the two letters that follow N.

4. Name the one letter that comes before the one letter that comes after K.

5. Say the ABCs in order.

BOOKTALKS : FAMOUS PEOPLE

Mae Jemison by Nancy Polette. Children's Press, 2004.

Mae Jemison was the first African-American woman to travel into space. Mae was born in 1956 in Decatur, Alabama, but grew up in Chicago, Illinois. When she was thirteen she saw the first astronauts walk on the moon. It was then she dreamed that she would be an astronaut, too. In high school, Mae liked math and science best. After college, she went to medical school and became a doctor. She applied to NASA to join the astronaut program and was accepted. In 1992 Mae traveled in space for eight days. As an engineer and a doctor Mae did experiments in space. She wanted to find a way to keep the astronauts from getting sick in space. She wanted to find a way to keep their bones strong. The shuttle went around the Earth 127 times. When Mae looked at the Earth from space, what do you think she saw? She saw Chicago! The place where her dream began.

John, Paul, George & Ben written and illustrated by Lane Smith. Hyperion, 2006.

This is a partly true and partly untrue story of four boys before they became famous men. John Hancock, Paul Revere, George Washington, and Ben Franklin. The author says that John Hancock's handwriting was so large that it took up the whole chalkboard; that Paul Revere was partly deaf so he had to shout at everyone; that George Washington's father admired his honesty in admitting he chopped down the cherry tree; and that Ben Franklin gave so much advice that people told him to be quiet.

On the last page the author tells us that John Hancock wrote his name in very large letters on the Declaration of Independence; that Paul Revere warned people that the British were coming; that George Washington did not chop down his father's cherry tree; and that Ben Franklin did write down his advice in *Poor Richard's Almanac*.

ABC POEM

Demonstrate your knowledge of ABC order by cutting the strips apart and putting them in ABC order by the first word on each strip.

If you are correct, you can read a poem about Mae Jemison.

Best in her class, that was Mae
Her dream to become an astronaut
Eager now to earn a place
College brought her a degree
Always learning, no time for play
Flying off into space
Giving her best, soon Mae got
Doctor Jemison she would be

TEST YOUR KNOWLEDGE

Cover the bottom half of the page.

Answer Yes or No to each of these statements.

Uncover the page to see correct answers.

1. _____ When John Hancock was a boy, he used the whole chalkboard to write his name.

2. _____ When Paul Revere was a boy, he belonged to a bell ringing club.

3. _____ Paul Revere made a midnight ride shouting, "The British are coming."

4. _____ George Washington wore silver buckles on his shoes.

John Hancock did not use the whole chalkboard to write his name but his name was the biggest name on the Declaration of Independence.

Paul Revere did belong to a bell ringing club. He also made a midnight ride to warn people that "The Redcoats [not the British] were coming."

Most of the men who lived in George Washington's time wore silver buckles on their shoes. George did, too.

LANGUAGE DEVELOPMENT

1. Patterns of written language must be stored in the brain before they can unlock print on a page.
2. A storehouse of language patterns is acquitted by hearing the written word read aloud.
3. Language patterns are stored more rapidly with the use of music or rhythm.
4. Repetition is essential. Young children are rarely bored by repetition.

ORAL PRACTICE

Add the missing words.

Choose from the following words:

man   boo   hoo   bit   hook   day   snake

Fishy, Fishy in the brook
Daddy caught him with a (1) _____
Mama fried him in a pan
Baby ate him like a (2) _____

Fishy, Fishy in the lake
Daddy caught him with a (3) _____
Mama caught a fishy, too
Baby cried and said (4) _____

Fishy, Fishy swam away
To come back another (5) _____
Mama cooked a goose instead
Baby cried and went to (6) _____

Answer Key: 1. hook 2. man 3. snake 4. boo hoo 5. day 6. bed

BOOKTALKS : ABOUT WORDS

Cat Up A Tree written and illustrated by John and Ann Hassett. Houghton Mifflin, 1998.

When Nana Quimby saw a cat up a tree she rang the firehouse. "Help," she cried. "Cat up a tree."

"Sorry," said the firehouse. "We do not catch cats up trees anymore. Call back if that cat starts playing with matches."

More and more cats climb up Nana Quimby's tree but no matter who she calls she gets no help. Each of these community helpers told her to call back if she had a different kind of problem: the police station, the pet shop, the zoo, the library, and City Hall. It seems that no one will help Nana Quimby.

After Nana Quimby rescues forty cats from the tree she gets a phone call from City Hall.

"Help," cried City Hall. "We have mice everywhere. We need a cat."

"Sorry," said Nana Quimby, "the cats do not catch mice anymore."

Max's Words by Kate Banks. Illus. by Boris Kulikov. Farrar, Straus & Giroux, 2006.

Max's brother collected stamps and coins. Max decided to collect words. He cut them out of magazines and newspapers. He collected large words and small words, food and color words and words that made him feel good. When his brothers added to their collections they had more stamps and coins. When Max added words to his collection he had sentences. With lots more words he would have a story. Max's brothers wanted to help with the story by moving words around. It was such an exciting story that they wanted to do another. They traded Max stamps and coins for more words. He gave them a few but kept the rest for himself. Now he could make lots of stories.

SENTENCE SUBSTITUTION

Read this sentence.

> The cat sat in the big tree.

Ask: What word could we use rather than tree?

> Examples: chair, car, bathtub

Read the new sentence.

> The cat sat in the big bathtub.

What word could we use rather than cat?

> Examples: dog, monkey, bear

Read the new sentence.

> The monkey sat in the big bathtub.

What word could we use instead of big?

> Examples: little, purple, wet

Read the new sentence.

> The monkey sat in the purple bathtub.

Continue by substituting words for cat and saw.

What word could we use in place of sat?

> Examples: danced, sang, ate

Read the new sentence.

> The monkey danced in the purple bathtub.

What other sentences can we make by changing words?

SENTENCE EXPANSION

Read this sentence.

Max collected words.

What describing words can be put in front of "words?"

Examples: funny, sad, crazy, silly

Read the new sentence.

Max collected _____ words.

What describing words can we put in from of Max?

Examples: busy, chubby, sweet

Read the new sentence.

_____ Max collected _____ words.

Make the sentence longer by taking away the period and adding words that begin with "which."

Examples: which made sentences, which he liked

Read the new sentence.

_____ Max collected _____ words which _____

_____

What other sentences can you make by adding different words?

ORIGINALITY

Originality is the ability to generate novel, non-traditional, or unexpected ideas.

Steps:

1. Determine and define the situation.

2. Define what is to be accomplished.

3. Brainstorm for original and unique ideas.

4. Interpret the ideas in clever and unique ways.

ORAL PRACTICE

Share: *The Little Old Lady Who Was Not Afraid of Anything* by Linda Williams. Illus. by Megan Lloyd. Harper Collins, 1986.

Once upon a time there was a little old lady who was not afraid of anything until one windy autumn night, while walking in the woods, she hears two shoes go CLOMP CLOMP. "I'm not afraid of you," says the little old lady. But the noises keep growing. Pants go wiggle, wiggle; a shirt goes shake, shake; gloves go clap, clap; a hat goes nod, nod. . . . and the little old lady who was not afraid of anything has the scare of her life.

Suppose instead of meeting clothing, the little old lady met parts of a bicycle on the path. What parts would she meet? What sound would each part make?

What else could she meet on the path?

BOOKTALKS : OLD TALES, NEW TWIST

The True Story of the Three Little Pigs by Jon Scieszka. Illus. by Lane Smith. Viking, 1989.

Here is the traditional *Three Little Pigs* tale retold by A. Wolf who wants readers to know what really happened. It seems that he wanted to make a birthday cake for his granny and needed to borrow some sugar from his closest neighbors, the pigs. However, A. Wolf had a bad cold and just before he could make his request for sugar, he sneezed so hard that he blew down the houses of the first two pigs. Not wanting to waste a perfectly good ham dinner, the wolf ate the pigs. However, when he tried to borrow sugar from the third pig with a house of bricks, the third pig called the police and the wolf ended up in jail. Not his fault at all, to hear him tell it.

Cinderella Skeleton by Robert D. San Souci. Illus. by David Catrow. Harcourt, 2000.

At first glance, Boneyard Acres might seem like any run-down, decayed graveyard. But if you look more closely, you'll meet Cinderella Skeleton, as sweetly foul as she can be. You might think that Cinderella Skeleton is the happiest ghoul in the land. But her two evil stepsisters treat her with scorn and leave her with all the housework and more. Enter Prince Charnel, the heartthrob of Halloween. As sure as bats fly and witches moan, Cinderella Skeleton steals his heart.

Out of the Egg written and illustrated by Tina Matthews. Houghton Mifflin, 2007.

Here is a new twist to the familiar tale of *The Little Red Hen*. In this story everything changes when the hard-working Red Hen lays a perfect white egg. Out of the egg comes a chick with very different ideas than those of its mother who does all the work. In a charming manner, chick chooses not to follow her mother's tradition of "going it alone."

ORIGINAL IDEAS

Look at these book titles. Answer each question as if you were the author. Give an answer you think no one else will give.

1. *Zuzu's Wishing Cake* by Linda Michelin. Houghton Mifflin, 2006. What is a wishing cake?

2. *The Cake that Mack Ate* by Rose Robart. Little Brown, 1986. Who is Mack?

3. *Flannel Kisses* by Linda Crotta Brennan. Houghton Mifflin, 1997. What are flannel kisses?

4. *A Very Full Morning* by Eva Montanari. Houghton Mifflin, 2006. What things will happen on a very full morning?

5. *When Owen's Mom Breathed Fire* by Pija Lindebom. R & S Books, 2006. Who is Owen? Who is Owen's mother? Why would she breathe fire?

6. *Brave Bitsy and the Bear* by Angela McAllister. Clarion, 2006. Who is Bitsy?

7. *Horton Hatches the Egg* by Dr. Seuss. Random House, 1940. Who is Horton? What hatches out of the egg?

AN ORIGINAL TALE

On each line add one or more words to create an original Cinderella tale.

There once was a girl named _____

who lived in a _____. The _____

was giving a _____. She could not

go because she had no _____. Late that night, a

_____ came and said to the girl, "Here are

_____. Now you can go to the

_____."

At the _____, she lost her _____

and ran back to her _____ leaving the _____

behind.

When the _____ found the _____,

it led him to the girl. He asked her to leave her home and go with him.

She said, "_____

_____

_____."

PATTERNING

Patterning is the repetition of words, sounds, images, or actions.

To recognize patterns:

1. Listen carefully for repeating sounds or words.
2. Look for the same action repeated over and over again.
3. Look for repeating lines or colors.
4. Identify the repeating pattern.

ORAL PRACTICE

Hickory Dickory

Hickory, dickory dot,
The mouse climbed in a pot,
Don't stop to stare
Here comes a _____
Hickory, dickory dot.

Hickory, dickory dole,
The mouse hid in a hole.
Then wouldn't you know,
Here comes a _____
Hickory, dickory dole.

Hickory, dickory day,
It's time to run away.
So pack your trunk,
Here comes a _____
Hickory, dickory day.

Follow the pattern.

Write your own Hickory, Dickory verse.

Answer Key: bear, crow, skunk

BOOKTALKS : PATTERNS

Brown Bear, Brown Bear, What Do You See? by Bill Martin, Jr. Holt, 1992.

The first line is repeated on every other page while a new animal is introduced. "Brown bear, brown bear, what do you see?" "I see a _____ looking at me." The end of the book introduces the teacher who sees happy children.

The Wheels on the Bus by Maryann Kovalski. Little Brown, 1987.

"The wheels on the bus go round and round, round and round, round and round. The wheels on the bus go round and round, all around the town." The pattern is repeated using the horn on the buss, the wipers on the bus, the people on the bus, the babies on the bus, and more.

Banjo Granny by Sarah Martin Busse and Jacqueline Briggs Martin. Illus. by Barry Root. Houghton Mifflin, 2006.

Granny who lived a long way away, sets out to see her new grandbaby but the trip is full of challenges. Granny hears that the new baby is "wiggly, jiggly, all-around giggly and tip over tumble for bluegrass music." Granny takes along her banjo case that contains not only her banjo for a fast river which slows down and listens. She played her banjo for a high mountain which leaned down and listened. Each song she plays is for her grandbaby who goes "wiggly, jiggly, all-around giggly and tip over tumble for bluegrass music." At last she reaches her grandbaby's house ready to play him a bluegrass tune. Children will enjoy chiming in the repeating pattern.

ON THE ROAD

Help Granny on her long trip to her grandbaby's house. Name animals or objects she **might** see on the way. They do not have to be from the story.

Sing to the tune of "The Farmer in the Dell."

A _____ was in the river

A _____ was in the river

That's what Banjo Granny saw

A _____ was in the river.

A _____ was on the mountain

A _____ was on the mountain

That's what Banjo Granny saw

A _____ was on the mountain.

A _____ was in the desert

A _____ was in the desert

That's what Banjo Granny saw

A _____ was in the desert.

A _____ was down the street

A _____ was down the street

That's what Banjo Granny saw

A _____ was down the street.

IN THE GARDEN

Use the names of different flowers in each verse.

Read the verses.

The _____ in the garden grows and grows,
Grows and grows, grows and grows.
The _____ in the garden grows and grows,
All day long.

The _____ in the garden dances in the wind,
Dances in the wind, dances in the wind.
The _____ in the garden dances in the wind,
All day long.

The _____ in the garden welcomes the bees,
Welcomes the bees, welcomes the bees.
The _____ in the garden welcomes the bees,
All day long.

The _____ in the garden loses its petals,
Loses its petals, loses its petals.
The _____ in the garden loses its petals,
All day long.

PHONEMIC AWARENESS

   Phonemic awareness is the ability to recognize the sounds of letters and to combine letter sounds to make words.

PHONEMIC AWARENESS MEANS:

1. **Rhyming**: Identify and form rhyming words.

2. **Sound Matching**: Identify similar word patterns (example: words beginning or ending with the same sound).

3. **Syllable Counting**: Count the syllables heard in words.

4. **Phoneme Blending**: Blend the sounds individual letters make to form words.

5. **Phoneme Isolation**: Identify the beginning, middle, and ending sounds in a word.

6. **Phoneme Addition/Deletion**: Add or delete a beginning, middle, or ending sound to a word.

7. **Phoneme Substitution**: Substitute a new sound for the beginning, middle, or ending sound of a word.

BOOKTALKS : ABC BOOKS

Albert B. Cub and Zebra by Anne Rockwell. Crowell, 1995.

On the A page, Albert's friend zebra has been abducted. To find him, Albert travels in an airplane and an automobile passing an accountant's sign, an Airedale, and a little girl crying in anguish. How many other A words can you find?

Potluck by Anne Shelby. Dial, 1998.

Each child is bringing one or more foods to a feast. The food and the way they bring the food (action verb) both begin with the first letter of the child's name. "Christine came with carrot cake and corn on the cob."

Alison's Zinnia by Anita Lobel. HarperCollins, 1998.

A fun book to use in a plant unit. "Beryl bought begonias for Crystal. Dawn dug daffodils for Emily." Study the pattern and write a similar sentence that begins with YOUR name. Try the same idea in a different setting.

The Hole by the Apple Tree by Nancy Polette. Greenwillow, 1989.

An ABC fairy tale adventure where Harold and his friends meet monsters in moats, question a queen, and try to save Snow White. Activity: Brainstorm all the fairy tale characters you can that begin with each letter of the alphabet. See how many you can find in this book.

Tomorrow's Alphabet by George Shannon. Illus. by Donald Crews. Greenwillow, 2002.

"A is for seed, tomorrow's apples."
"B is for egg, tomorrow's birds."
Take two of the words from this book and use them in this pattern: Eggs are just eggs until they hatch and then they become birds. Scraps are just scraps until they are sewn together and then they become a quilt.

SINGING BLENDS

Phoneme Blending

Blend the sounds individual letters make to form words.

Tune: "Old MacDonald Had a Farm"

S/T are the letters that make this blend

Stoop, stop, stair

With an S/T here and an S/T there

S/T, S/T everywhere

S/T are the letters that make these blends

Stoop, stop stair.

C/H are the letters that make this blend

Cheese, chop, chair

With an C/H here and a C/H there

C/H, C/H everywhere

C/H are the letters that make these blends

Cheese, chop, chair.

Add more verses using: B/R, C/R, F/R, G/R, B/L, F/L, S/K, S/P, W/R

CHANGING LETTERS

Tune: "If You're Happy and You Know It"

A /D/ in the front of ATE makes _____ (DATE)

A /T/ in the front of APE makes _____ (TAPE)

Add a /B/ to URN get _____ (BURN)

Add a /T/, and it's your _____ (TURN)

Adding letters makes new words

For us to hear.

A /C/ in front of lock makes _____ (CLOCK)

An /S/ in front of HOT makes _____ (SHOT)

Take away the /P/ in POT

Add an /H/, the POT gets _____ (HOT)

Adding letters makes new words

For us to hear.

PLANNING

Planning means organizing a method for achieving a specific outcome or goal.

Steps:

1. State the problem, project, or task.

2. List and locate needed materials.

3. List steps necessary to complete the project or task.

4. Identify problems.

5. Follow the planning steps.

ORAL PRACTICE

Project: To make a peanut butter sandwich.

1. What materials are needed?

2. List the steps in making the sandwich.

3. Suppose your guests like smooth peanut butter and you have only crunchy peanut butter. What will you do?

BOOKTALKS : BOOKS BY TOMIE DEPAOLA

Strega Nona by Tomie dePaola. Scholastic, 1975.

In the town of Calabria, there lived an old lady everyone called Strega Nona, which meant "Grandma Witch." The town would go to see her if they had troubles. Since Strega Nona was getting old she needed help. So she put up a help-wanted sign in the town square. Big Anthony who didn't pay attention went to see her and started working for Strega Nona. But there was one condition, he must never touch her cooking pot. However, in her absence he says the magic words that cause the pot to cook. Pasta is everywhere! Unfortunately, Big Anthony does not know the words to turn the pot off. Imagine what happens when Strega Nona returns!

Strega Nona's Magic Lessons by Tomie dePaola. Harcourt, 1982.

Strega Nona had two pupils for her magic lessons. One was Bambolona, the town baker's daughter, and the other was "Antonia," who was really Strega Nona's helper, Big Anthony, dressed up like a girl. Bambolona learned quickly and well. Big Anthony was not a very good student. When Strega Nona gives Bambolona a book containing more magic spells, Big Anthony tries to surprise Strega Nona by learning magic on his own. All he manages to do is turn her into a frog, which did not please her at all. Big Anthony again learns an important lesson…not to do magic until you have learned very well.

The Legend of the Indian Paintbrush by Tomie dePaola. Putnam, 1988.

A very small Plains Indian boy longs to grow tall and strong and to join the brave warriors and hunters. But he was too small to keep up with the other boys and was not strong at all. He was not consoled by the wise shaman of the tribe who told him that he would be remembered by the People for another reason. After a time, as the boy grew, he had a vision in which an old man and a young girl spoke to him, telling him that it was his task to paint the deeds of the warriors and the visions of the shamans. The boy then became the recorder of the tribe's history but was not satisfied with the dull colors with which he had to work. The vision came again and he was told here to find his colors. He followed the directions and found brushes filled with paint that allowed him to create a sunset in vivid color. When his painting was finished, he left the brushes behind and the next morning the hill was filled with color as the brushes had taken root in the earth.

PLAN AN AUTHOR BIRTHDAY PARTY

Tomie dePaola

1. Decide on the author. (Example: Tomie dePaola)

2. Decide who will be invited.

   _____

3. Decide on the day and the time.

   _____

4. Who will prepare the invitations? What will they look like?

   _____

5. List and locate the author's books. Problem: Where can you find books not in your library?

   _____

6. Where can we find information to share about the author?

   _____

7. What decorations are needed? Who will make the decorations?

   _____

8. What games will be played? Who will prepare or obtain the games?

   _____

9. Decide on refreshments. Problem: Who will prepare refreshments? What cost is involved? Where will the money come from?

   _____

10. Who will clean up after the party?

    _____

AUTHOR BIRTHDAY PARTY GAME

How many titles by Tomie dePaola can you find and underline?

Oliver Button is a sissy. You can imagine how he felt, eating pancakes for breakfast, when the radio said T-Rex is missing! Oliver lived at 26 Fairmount Avenue with his grandmother, Nana Upstairs. Nana Downstairs was his other grandmother.

Oliver decided to take Strega Nona's magic lessons to make the T-Rex disappear. "An art lesson would be better," his mother said. "You can wipe the T-Rex off the canvas after painting it."

Kit and Kat, Oliver's other neighbors asked Oliver where he was going.

"I'm on my way to see Strega Nona. Her magic will keep me and my baby sister safe from the T-Rex."

"You should go see Big Anthony and the magic ring he wears," Kit called. "You can rub the ring and wish the T-Rex away. If you can't find Big Anthony, ask Finn M'Coul, the giant of Knockmanny Hill to help.

Titles to find: *Oliver Button is a Sissy; Pancakes for Breakfast; T-Rex is Missing; 26 Fairmount Avenue; Nana Upstairs, Nana Downstairs; Strega Nona's Magic Lessons; Art Lesson; Kit and Kat; Baby Sister; Strega Nona; Big Anthony and the Magic Ring; Finn M'Coul, the Giant of Knockmanny Hill.*

PREDICTING

Predicting is to forecast or anticipate what might happen based on evidence.

Steps:

1. Clarify what is to be predicted.

2. Analyze data to find a basis for predicting.

3. Make a tentative prediction.

4. Consider related data and modify predictions as necessary.

ORAL PRACTICE

Predict:

What will happen when the sky turns gray and big clouds form in the sky? Why?

What will happen to a snowman when the sun comes out? Why?

What will happen if a skunk wanders into the schoolyard at recess? Why?

BOOKTALKS : ANIMAL CLASSICS

The Story of Ferdinand by Munro Leaf. Illus. by Robert Lawson. Viking Press, 1984.

Ferdinand is a gentle bull who likes to sit and smell the flowers. When men come to pick the fiercest bull for the bullfight, Ferdinand is stung by a bee. He stomped and roared and puffed and snorted. The men thought he was the fiercest bull and chose him. What do you think will happen when Ferdinand enters the bull ring?

Frederick by Leo Lionni. Pantheon, 1967.

The mouse family is preparing for winter, gathering corn, nuts, wheat, and straw. They worked day and night to store enough food to last through the cold winter months. But Frederick did not gather food or straw. He gathered colors and words which the other mice thought were foolish things to gather. Then winter comes and when the cold seeps through the granary and the food supply is almost gone. What do you think Frederick will do?

Katy No-Pocket by Emmy Payne. Houghton Mifflin, 1944.

Imagine a mother kangaroo without a pocket. Where will she carry her baby? This is Katy No-Pocket's problem. Her baby, Freddy, needs a warm pocket to ride in when Katy goes from one place to another. All the other mother kangaroos have pockets for their babies so Katy has to find one. Where do you suppose Katy will find a pocket?

Rainbow Fish by Marcus Pfister. North-South Books, 1995.

Rainbow Fish had no equal in the ocean for beauty. He is talked about and greatly admired by all the other sea creatures for his scales sparkle and shine with many colors—purple, green, silver, and blue. The more he was admired, the prouder he felt. Then came a day when a very small blue fish asked Rainbow Fish for one of his scales. Predict what Rainbow Fish will do.

TELL WHAT WILL HAPPEN. WHY?

WHAT WOULD HAPPEN IF . . .

Share: *The Very Hungry Caterpillar* by Eric Carle. Philomel, 1969.

This caterpillar was very hungry so he ate everything he could find, including cake and pickles. He ate and ate and ate. Predict what will happen to the caterpillar.

Share: *The Tale of Peter Rabbit* by Beatrix Potter. Frederick Warne, 1905.

Before going out one day, Peter's mother, Mrs. Rabbit, tells her four bunnies they must not go into Mr. McGregor's garden where their father once strayed and ended up in a pie. Peter being an adventurous sort, heads straight to the garden. Predict what will happen to Peter.

Share: *Blueberries for Sal* by Robert McCloskey. Illus. by Betty Fraser. Viking, 1978.

A mother and her child go berry picking on Blueberry Hill. Mother wants to can the berries for winter. A mother bear and her cub go berry eating on Blueberry Hill at the same time. Mother Bear wants her cub to eat lots of berries to get ready for winter. Imagine the surprised mothers when they turn around to find each other's children behind them! Predict what will happen next.

PROBLEM SOLVING

In **problem solving**, solutions to a problem are weighed using selected criteria.

> **Steps:**
>
> 1. Identify and define the problem.
>
> 2. List important facts about the problem or situation.
>
> 3. List alternative solutions to the problem.
>
> 4. List criteria for appraising each solution.
>
> 5. Apply criteria to each solution, giving a numerical value to each. A value of one is low, a value of three is high.
>
> 6. Total the values for each alternative.
>
> 7. State the solution.
>
> 8. Devise a plan to gain acceptance of the solution by others.

BOOKTALKS : WILD ANIMALS

Annie and the Wild Animals written and illustrated by Jan Brett. Houghton Mifflin, 1995.

It had been a long winter and the snow was falling again. Annie could not find her cat, Taffy, anywhere. She waited and waited for Taffy to return but Taffy was not to be seen. So Annie decided to make some corn cakes and leave them at the edge of the woods to attract another small animal to be her pet. Annie could not believe the animals that appeared…a moose, a wildcat, a bear, and a stag. None of these animals would make a good pet. They snarled and roared even louder when Annie ran out of corn meal and had no corn cakes to give them. What will Annie do?

The Biggest Bear by Lynd Ward. Houghton Mifflin, 1952. Renewed 1980.

Everyone in Johnny Orchard's town had huge bearskins hanging on the sides of their barns. Everyone's, that is, except for Johnny's barn. Their barn didn't have one, and this was very humiliating for Johnny. He was determined to have a skin hanging on this barn as well, so Johnny went hunting for his own bear—the biggest bear. Johnny did come back with his bear, but it was far from big, in fact it was a little cub. But that little cub brought big trouble as it grew bigger and bigger. It went places it was not supposed to go. Neighbors complained that the bear was destroying their property. It was time to get rid of the bear. What will Johnny do?

ANNIE'S PET

Annie's cat, Taffy, has disappeared. Annie lives near the woods. Annie wants a new pet. How can Annie find a new pet?

List three ideas. One idea is listed for you.

Rank each idea   1 = no   2 = maybe   3 = yes

IDEAS	FAST	EASY	SAFE FOR ANNIE	WILL WORK	TOTAL
Put out food	2	2	3	2	9

The best idea for Annie to try to get a new pet is

_____

_____

_____

_____

_____

WHAT TO DO WITH A BIG BEAR

Johnny found the bear when it was a small cub. Johnny takes such good care of the bear that it grows into a big bear. Johnny's neighbor tells Johnny he must find a new home for the bear. What will he do?

List three ideas. One idea is listed for you.

Rank each idea   1 = no   2 = maybe   3 = yes

IDEAS	FAST	BEAR WILL STAY	SAFE FOR THE BEAR	BEAR GONE FOR GOOD	TOTAL
Turn the bear loose	2	1	3	1	7

The best idea way to find a new home for the bear is

_____

_____

_____

QUESTIONING: HIGHER ORDER

Higher order questions can have more than one right answer.

QUANTITY QUESTIONS

How many...

How many ways...

List all... [parts, uses, ways]

COMPARE/CONTRAST QUESTIONS

How is _____ like _____?

How is _____ different from _____?

FEELINGS / OPINIONS QUESTIONS

Would you rather...

How did or would you feel about...

"WHAT WOULD HAPPEN IF" QUESTIONS

What if...

What would happen...

"IF YOU WERE" QUESTIONS

Suppose that...

What if you...

ORAL PRACTICE

How many animal stories can you name?

How is *The Cat in the Hat* like Horton in *Horton Hatches the Egg*? How are the two stories different?

Would you rather play the part of Charlotte or Wilbur in a class play of *Charlotte's Web*? Why?

What would happen if there were no books?

Suppose that you could make things move by looking at them. What would you do?

BOOKTALKS : ON STAGE

The Gold Miner's Daughter by Jackie Mims Hopkins. Illus. by Jon Goodell. Peachtree Books, 2006.

Pa and Gracie live deep in the heart of gold mining country, but their mine is dry, not a nugget to be found. To make matters worse, if they can't find a way to pay the rent by sunset to mean old Mr. Bigglebottom, he will take back their land and house and force Gracie to marry him.

Gracie hitches up her mule and heads into town hoping to find the money somewhere. She passes three pigs, tied to train tracks by Mr. Bigglebottom because they couldn't pay their rent. The storekeeper told Gracie that the goose that laid golden eggs was gone. She had no luck finding a spinning wheel that could spin straw into gold. She returns to Pa empty handed. Then who shows up but Mr. Bigglebottom demanding the rent. Will Gracie and Pa lose their home? Will Gracie have to marry Mr. Bigglebottom? Who knows? Perhaps there is unexpected wealth just beneath their feet.

Ella Sets the Stage by Carmela and Steven D'Amico. Arthur A. Levine Books, 2006.

All of the elephant children on Elephant Island are excited. The school is having a talent show and all of Ella's friends plan to be part of the show. Belinda will dance. Daisy will sing. Frankie will put on a puppet show. Tiki and Lola will do acrobatics. Ella is sad because she has no talent to share. On the night of the show she takes cupcakes and lemonade for her friends. She sews a rip in Belinda's tutu. She uses her hat to catch a disappearing monkey. She helps each performer so that the show is a great success. When prizes are given out there is a special prize for Ella. Her talent was being a special friend to everyone, a talent she did not know she had.

WHAT IF...

What if you found yourself in a gold mine?

And you could hear _____

And you could see _____

And you could smell _____

You would pick up a

_____ and

_____

What if you found yourself at a talent show?

And you can hear _____

And you can see

_____

And you can smell

_____

You would step on stage and _____

_____

COMPARE / CONTRAST

A gold mine is like a supermarket because

_____

A gold mine is different from a supermarket because

_____

A train track is like a road because

_____

A train track is different from a road because

_____

A spinning wheel is like a car because

_____

A spinning wheel is different from a car because

_____

An egg is like an orange because

_____

An egg is different from an orange because

_____

Oil is like a pot of coffee because

_____

Oil is different from a pot of coffee because

_____

RESEARCH FOR BEGINNERS

Young children do well with **research** if given a clear understanding of what is to be found and a pattern to follow in reporting the research.

Steps:

1. Present the research task. (Finding information about an animal)

2. Give specific items to be found. (What the animal eats, where it lives, what it looks like, and what it does)

3. Tell how many items must be listed under each heading.

4. Provide books/articles on the child's reading level that contain the needed information.

5. Use the information in a song [*Tune*: "London Bridge"]

   Woodchucks have short legs and brown fur

   Woodchucks eat grass and hay

   Woodchucks whistle and climb trees

   And live in the forest

BOOKTALKS : NATURE

Isn't It Strange? by Nancy Polette. Kaeden Books, 2005.

When nature makes magic, many things change. "Deep deep down in a swampy bog, a tadpole grows legs and becomes a frog. In the garden hour by hour, a tiny seed bursts and becomes a flower." How many other things can children name that change from one form to another? Beautiful photographs show each magical change.

Growing Like Me by Anne Rockwell. Illus. by Holly Keller. Harcourt, Inc., 2001.

A delightful book that shows change in nature and relates the changes to the reader with the phrase "just like me." "Here in the meadow, by the woods and the pond, everything is growing, just like me. White blossoms will grow into berries, black and juicy and sweet."

For more books about change, see: *How Things Grow* series by Jane Kottke. Children's Press, 2000.

A level one reading series that includes: *From Acorn to Oak Tree, From Caterpillar to Moth, From Egg to Robin, From Seed to Dandelion, From Seed to Pumpkin*, and *From Tadpole to Frog*.

White Bear, Ice Bear by Joanne Ryder. Illus. by Michael Rotham. Morrow, 1989.

Experience one day in the life of a polar bear. The book begins with a child who awakens in the morning and goes outside to become a polar bear. The child lives the life of the bear for one day as it moves along the icy peaks with only its small black nose to be seen. It hunts by finding a hole in the ice, but the seal, its prey, quickly swims away. Near the end of the day the bear senses a familiar smell and peeks through a window at another world waiting. It pushes open the door and enters the house as the child once again, "hungry and happy to be home." This is one of a series of books about wild animals, beautifully told and illustrated. Others in the series include: *Winter Whale* and *Jaguar in the Rain Forest*.

THINGS THAT CHANGE

Complete these sentences:

A tiny seed becomes a _____.

From an egg there comes a _____.

From caterpillar to _____.

A green tadpole becomes a _____.

A brown acorn becomes a _____.

Use the information in a song. [*Tune*: "Mary Had a Little Lamb"]

Example:

A *tiny seed* becomes a *flower*
Becomes a *flower*, becomes a *flower*
A *tiny seed* becomes a *flower*
And it *grows* in the *garden*.

A _____ becomes a _____

Becomes a _____, becomes a _____

A _____ becomes a _____

And it _____   _____
           (does what?)   (where?)

WOODLAND ANIMALS

1. Name four woodland animals

    _____   _____

    _____   _____

2. What might you see or hear each doing?

    _____   _____

    _____   _____

Use the words in this pattern.

     Walking through the woods what do I see?

     I see a rabbit hopping for me

In the _____

What do I see? I see a _____

_____ at / for me.

Between the _____

What do I see? I see a _____

_____ at / for me.

Behind the _____

What do I see? I see a _____

_____ at / for me.

On the _____

What do I see?   I see a _____

_____ at / for me.

REVERSIBLE THINKING

Reversible thinking is the ability to think back through a story or an operation from the end to the beginning.

Steps:

1. Read or tell a story or situation that includes sequential steps.

2. Retell the events, steps, or story in reverse order, from the end to the beginning.

ORAL PRACTICE

1. Describe in detail the route from the classroom to the lunchroom or school library. Then tell how to reverse the trip to return to the classroom.

2. Describe an accident you have had from the end of the accident to the beginning.

3. Describe the process of feeding your pet from the thing you do last to the thing you do first.

4. Recount a day in your life from the last thing you do to the first thing you do.

BOOKTALKS : FROM LAST TO FIRST

If You Give a Mouse a Cookie by Laura Joffe Numeroff. Illus. by Felicia Bond. HarperCollins, 1985.

Giving a mouse a cookie should be a simple matter but it does lead to complications in this story. Cookies and milk go together so, of course, the mouse has to have some milk. In wiping the milk off his whiskers, he realizes that the whiskers need a trim and after trimming he sweeps up with a broom. Before he can have a nap he must have a story and a story is so exciting that he must draw a picture of it. When the picture is displayed on the refrigerator the mouse realizes that he is hungry again and must have a cookie with, of course, a glass of milk to go with it.

The End by David LaRochelle. Illus. by Richard Egielski. Scholastic, 2007.

A story is told from the end to the beginning when a prince and princess live happily ever after because the princess throws lemonade on the prince because his beard is on fire. He had been tickling a dragon to stop its crying because the dragon was frightened by 100 bunny rabbits escaping from an enormous tomato hit by a flying teacup thrown by a giant in a temper tantrum because his cook did not make lemon cheesecake for dessert. She could not buy any lemons at the store because the princess had bought all the lemons to make lemonade.

I WONDER WHY?

A Backwards Turkey

I wonder why they

    Eat the turkey

    Serve the turkey

    Slice the turkey

    Baste the turkey

    Bake the turkey

    Stuff the turkey

    Thaw the turkey

    Buy the turkey

When I could have spaghetti instead?

> Here are the steps in preparing a turkey from the last step to the first step.
>
> Below, list the steps in making a peanut butter sandwich from last to first.

A Peanut Butter Sandwich

I wonder why I

_____

_____

_____

_____

_____

When I could have _____ instead?

A BACKWARDS STORY

Read the backwards story.

Grandma scooted out!
Then they heard a (1) _____
She hid under the bed.
Grandma had used her (2) _____

The wolf ran far away
A hunter came to (3) _____
"It's time to swallow you down"
The wolf said with a (4) _____

"You have a wolf-like head"
So the young girl (5) _____ _____
And walked across the floor
She entered through the (6) _____

The wolf would get there first
Hearing this outburst
I'm taking her some food
I don't mean to be (7) _____

For Grandma's feeling ill
Let me pass, if you (8) _____
A wolf stopped her to talk
Along her forest (9) _____

For Grandma, sick in bed
She carried soup and (10) _____
Along a woodland route
A little girl set (11) _____

Add the missing rhyming words.
frown
walk
shout
rude
head
will
stay
bread
out
said
door

Answer Key: 1. shout 2. head 3. stay 4. frown 5. said 6. door
7. rude 8. will 9. walk 10. bread 11. out

SEQUENCING

Sequencing requires placing items in the order in which they occur.

Steps:

1. Choose items or events to be sequenced.

2. Consider the relationship between the items of events.

3. Order the events or items according to an ascending or descending relationship.

   Size: from small to large or large to small

   Value: from less to more or more to less

   Time: from now to later or later to now

   Position: from near to far or far to near

   Alphabetical: from A to Z or Z to A

   Events: from first to last or last to first

BOOKTALKS : PLAY BALL!

Batter Up Wombat by Helen Lester. Illus. by Lynn Munsinger. Houghton Mifflin, 2006.

> Last year the Champs finished last in the Wildlife League. This year they were determined to do better. The team mistakes a wombat for a "whambat" and they think they have found a big hitter. The wombat was happy to join the team although he didn't know anything about baseball. He thought a bat was an animal; a pitcher held milk; home plate was a dish; and a foul was a chicken. When he was told he was the next hitter up, he was unhappy because he didn't want to hit anyone. When teammates told him to "run home," he thought they meant to run to Australia, a very long way away. Just as it looks like the game is lost, a tornado swoops down on the field. Wombat shows his real talent for digging and digs a tunnel to save both teams.

Pecorino Plays Ball by Alan Madison. Illus. by AnnaLaura Cantone. Atheneum, 2006.

> Pecorino Sasquatch is a boy who does everything backwards. He eats candy at Thanksgiving and turkey on Halloween. When his mother signs him up for Little League, he has never played baseball and thinks it might be fun. He can't catch a fly ball and strikes out at bat. The uniforms are confusing, saying things like "Alone we sell oxes" and "hit me". But in the end Pecorino saves the day for the team when he trips on his oversized uniform shirt and a fly ball lands in his mitt. Baseball, he thinks, is a pretty fun game after all.

TELL THE STORY I

Cut out the story strips and put them in order to tell the story.

1. The umpire says wombat is OUT!
2. Wombat joins the team.
3. Wombat's teammates are disappointed.
4. Wombat digs a tunnel.
5. Wombat hits the ball.
6. Wombat shows up on the ballfield.
7. Wombat saves his teammates.
8. Wombat thinks a bat is an animal.
9. Wombat steals third base and leaves the field.
10. A tornado heads for the ballfield.

Answer Key: 6, 2, 8, 5, 9, 1, 3, 10, 4, 7

TELL THE STORY II

Cut out the story strips and put them in order to tell the story.

1. He missed his first catch.
2. The ball smashed into his mitt.
3. It is Pecorino's first day of Little League.
4. He struck out at bat.
5. Pecorino's catch won the game.
6. He tripped on his long shirt.
7. He put on his extra large uniform.
8. He found and chewed bubble gum.

Answer Key: 3, 7, 1, 4, 8, 6, 2, 5

VOCABULARY

Thinking, speaking, and writing ability is only as strong as the words and patterns stored in the brain.

BUILDING WORD POWER

Concept Ladder for Concrete Nouns

Word _____

Kind of? _____

Member of? _____

Made of?_____

Used for? _____

Origin of? _____

BOOKTALKS : BIG WORDS

Cookies by Amy Krouse Rosenthal. Illus. by Jane Dyer. HarperCollins, 2006.

Each page introduces a new vocabulary word using cookies to explain the word. Greedy means taking all the cookies for myself. Honest means "The butterfly didn't really take the cookie. I took the cookie." Other words made clear with the cookie theme are: trust-worthy, courageous, patient, proud, modest, respect, fair, unfair, optimistic, pessimistic, polite, envy, loyal, and regret. These same words could be explained using a ball, a bicycle, a cup, or any other object. In addition, other words can be introduced using the same idea.

Winston, The Book Wolf by Marni McGee. Illus. by Ian Beck. Walker & Company, 2006.

A wolf is chased from the library because he chews up the books. He found words to be a tastier treat than meat. A little girl named Rosie befriends the wolf and shows him that "eating words" with the eyes can be much more fun. She reads story after story to the wolf and soon the wolf learned to read and could enjoy the stories by himself. When he wanted more books, Rosie dresses the wolf in her grandmother's clothes and takes him to the library. Not only can he borrow books, he becomes the library's favorite storyteller.

MYSTERY BOOK TITLES

Some words in these titles have been changed into bigger words. Guess the names of the titles.

1. The Kitten in a Head Covering

2. A Trio of Small Swine

3. A Successful Small Locomotive

4. A Small Cottage

5. 24 Hours of White Flakes Coming Down

6. A Train Headed for a Very Cold Place

7. The Snoozing Beautiful Woman

8. Kitten Wearing Knee High Foot Coverings

Answer Key: 1. *The Cat in the Hat* 2. *Three Little Pigs* 3. *Little Engine that Could* 4. *Little House* 5. *Snowy Day* 6. *Polar Express* 7. *Sleeping Beauty* 8. *Puss in Boots*

A SPELLING GAME

Use these letters to make the missing words.

G P N S R I

1. The wolf who liked to eat words had to first ___ ___ ___ the pages from the book.

2. Take away one letter and add one letter to make the missing word. If the wolf loses a button from his shirt, he will need a ___ ___ ___.

3. Take away one letter and add two letters to tell what a doorbell does. ___ ___ ___ ___

4. Move the letters around to tell how the wolf showed he was happy. ___ ___ ___ ___

5. Take away one letter and add one letter. When the wolf turns round and round he starts to ___ ___ ___ ___.

6. Use all of the letters to make a word that tells the time of the year the wolf likes best. ___ ___ ___ ___ ___

Answer Key: 1. rip 2. pin 3. ring 4. grin 5. spin 6. spring

Title / Author Index

About the Author

NANCY POLETTE is a well-known author, presenter, and speaker who has written many books for Teacher Ideas Press and Libraries Unlimited. She is Professor of Education at Lindenwood University in St. Charles, Missouri.